TRIUMPH OVER TEMPTATION

TRIUMPH OVER TEMPTATION

Encounters at the Testing Tree

by
Ward Patterson

illustrated by
Michael Streff

STANDARD PUBLISHING
Cincinnati, Ohio   39976

Unless otherwise noted, Scripture references are from the New American Standard Bible, ©The Lockman Foundation, 1960, 1962, 1963, 1968, 1971, 1972, 1975, 1977, and are used by permission.

Library of Congress Cataloging in Publication Data

Patterson, Ward.
    Triumph over temptation.

    1. Temptation—Biblical teaching.   I. Title.
BS680.T43P37   1984   248.4   84-36
ISBN 0-87239-730-0

Sharing the thoughts of his own heart, the author may express views that are not entirely consistent with those of the publisher.

TABLE OF
CONTENTS

Introduction

TEMPTATION
And the Company It Keeps

Temptation, to most of us, is a dirty word. It keeps company with rebellion, immorality, sin, and Satan. It lurks in the darkness, waiting to use our weaknesses to waste us. It lures us into the valley of sin and dumps us in the *gehenna* of guilt.

Temptation, in our minds, is Satan's brainchild. It is the Deceiver's great put-on, his great cunning confidence scheme, his lie-baited trap deceptively leading us into captivity to his devilish designs. Satan is a hustler and temptation is his game. He's after our shirts, souls, and eyelashes.  Temptation is Satan's invitation to play a rigged and ruinous game. It's the set-up that leads to the kill.

Looking at temptation in this light, we wonder whether James were suffering from a sunstroke when he wrote, "Count it all joy when ye fall into divers temptations" (James 1:2, KJV). That sounds a little weird to our ears, and not just because we have to look up "divers" in the dictionary. How can James say that we should regard ourselves as supremely happy when we become Satan's mark? It sounds like the sort of thing you would hear from a fellow who recommends skydiving without a parachute.

The problem, however, belongs to us, not James. The fact is that our English word, *tempt*, in its current usage, no

7

longer corresponds with the Greek and Hebrew words commonly translated by it in the King James Version. That is not the fault of either James—James the Lord's brother or James the King of England. It is just one of those things that happens with the passage of three or four hundred years. That is why newer versions, particularly the New American Standard Bible, will be cited in these studies.

None of us enjoys "trials" and "tests" much more than we enjoy "temptations," but it is a little easier to get James' drift when we hear him saying, "Consider it all joy, my brethren, when you encounter various trials, knowing that the testing of your faith produces endurance" (James 1:2, 3, NASB). The Greek word translated *trials* in the New American Standard Bible, and *temptation* in the King James, derives from *peirazo*. This is not the name of some Italian pasta. It is

the Greek word that conveys the idea of putting something or someone to the test in order to assess real value, endurance, or strength. *Peirazo* is what they do in Detroit when they put the new model through its paces to detect flaws in its design or workmanship. *Peirazo* is what they do to the spacecraft before it is launched and to the astronaut before he qualifies to man it. The Greeks had neither Cadillacs nor countdowns, but they knew the best way to discover the value and worth of a thing was to *peirazo* it, to put it to the test. If the test were particularly severe, the Greeks used the word *ekpeirazo*.

The Hebrew words used in the Old Testament were similar to the Greek. *Bachan* and *nasah* both mean to prove, try, or test. The Hebrews compared God's testing of man with the way precious metals were refined by heat. "The refining pot is for silver and the furnace for gold, but the Lord tests hearts" (Proverbs 17:3). The purification element is strong in the Hebrew word *tsaraph* (Psalm 66:10).

A little Greek and Hebrew in the introduction always adds a touch of class to a book, but it is included here primarily to get across the idea that temptation, in the Scriptural sense, has possibilities for holiness as well as for sinfulness. Temptation, testing, need not be the initiatory rite to sin. It too often is, for we so frequently cave in at the point of testing. But it can just as well be a proving ground for righteousness. Scripture indicates that testing is designed by our all-wise Creator to be beneficial for our free identity and inner spiritual development rather than to be destructive for our souls.

Temptation is not the same thing as sin. It may well prove to be an occasion for sin, but it can be an occasion for over-coming—for victorious trust in God. Jesus was tempted, but He did not sin (Hebrews 4:15). In this, as in all other things, He gives us the perfect example.

T ≠ S
Temptation does NOT = Sin

Tests are all around us. We are constantly encouraged to put theory to the test of experience. Research and development scientists labor to refine their techniques of testing everything we consume, whether drugs, deodorants, detergents, or diapers. We consider product testing to be essential to the improvement of our technology. The academic community also thrives on it. We feel that it is necessary that doctors pass certain tests and achieve certain standards before they are licensed to practice medicine. Yet, to most students, a test is about as welcome as a toothache. Tests, they are convinced, are designed by sadistic teachers whose main objective in life is to make students feel stupid.

Is a test designed to make us fail? Or is it designed to give us an opportunity for demonstrating our mastery of needed knowledge and skills? The test may do either. Its outcome depends largely on the student. Some students actually look forward to tests. They have a peculiar habit of studying hard and knowing the material. A test, to them, is a desirable challenge rather than a debilitating catastrophe.

Our lives are filled with personal tests. How should we view them? Are they to be considered as unwelcome intruders into an otherwise tranquil existence? Or are they woven into the fabric of creation by the all-wise and all-loving Creator whose works always pass the test for goodness?

The Bible, not surprisingly, speaks a great deal about the testing of "temptation." Our ancient ancestors, Adam and Eve, were given a special testing place in the good garden that God provided for them (Genesis 2:17). God tested Abraham with His incongruous command to offer his only son, Isaac, as a sacrifice (Genesis 22:1). God tested the children of Israel in the wilderness of Sinai (Deuteronomy 8:2, 3) and the kings of Israel in their wars (2 Chronicles 20:30). He allowed Job to be tested (Job 1:12; 2:6). The disciples of Jesus were tested (Luke 22:31), as was Jesus himself (Matthew 4:1-11).

In the garden that was in Eden, the tree of the knowledge of good and evil was the locus of testing. That particular tree was the tree for the opportunity of experientially knowing good. It was also, at the same time, the tree for the opportunity of experientially knowing evil. Each of us today, as we confront situations for spiritual testing, stand at our own testing trees. In the studies that follow, we will give attention to both defeats suffered and victories won at the testing trees of Biblical history.

The Bible begins with a record of man's tragic failure in the garden in Eden. It continues with the chronicles of both failure and victory. It climaxes with unqualified victory in the person of Jesus, whose ultimate testing tree was the cross itself.

Our purpose for these studies is not merely academic. We are talking of life and death matters. What we do at the testing trees of our lives is of eternal significance. We study, not to pass a test that might be given at the end of this course. We study to pass the test of life itself.

> Why should any living mortal, or any man,
> Offer complaint in view of his sins?
> Let us examine and probe our ways,
> And let us return to the Lord (Lamentations 3:39, 40).

Chapter One

MAN
At the Testing Tree
(Genesis 3)

The testing tree stood in the garden. On it God had placed a sign, "Unfit for Human Consumption." Genesis 2:16, 17 says, "And the Lord God commanded the man, saying, 'From any tree in the garden you may eat freely; but from the tree of the knowledge of good and evil you shall not eat, for in the day that you eat from it you shall surely die.' " That tree was no accident. It was not a malicious, alien freak of nature that somehow rooted its way into an otherwise perfect paradise. The *Lord* planted that tree, along with the others (Genesis 2:8). Like all the others it was good and beautiful and designed for the benefit of man. It would never have become a tree of death had man not voluntarily decided to make it so.

Why was there such a tree in the garden? We are not told explicitly, but our understanding of the nature of man in relation to the nature of that tree gives us some clues. It seems that God created man a free being for companionship with himself. Man could not have been truly free without an option. Had man stood firm in his obedience to God, that tree would have become a symbol to us of man's righteousness, as no other tree in the garden ever could have. As it is, that tree has become the symbol of man's rebellion, as no other tree in the garden ever could have. It is written in history and it is written in our natures that man failed at the testing tree.

The tree was good by design, but it was capable of being turned into evil. That's the reason Satan was so interested in it. That is Satan's chief sport, turning things that are good by design into evil. He does it with human sexuality all the time. He does it with our other God-given human impulses and urges. He does it with all testing opportunities.

How does he do it? His method is the "big lie" and the twisted half truth. He poses as our friendly informant, the revealer of the real "truth" about things. He promises to free us from God's restrictions and expand our consciousness. His method was the same with Eve.

The word translated "serpent" in Genesis 3:1 may mean "shining one." If so, Satan was using one of his favorite disguises. Paul, when writing to the Corinthian church, warned that "Satan disguises himself as an angel of light" (2 Corinthians 11:14). While it is not our purpose here to go into an exhaustive study of Satan, we ought to know enough about him to recognize his basic (Or should we say "base"?) nature. He is the enemy of both God and man (Matthew 13:39), the adversary (1 Peter 5:8), the tempter (Matthew 4:3; 1 Thessalonians 3:5), the father of lies (John 8:44), the deceiver (Revelation 12:9), a murderer (John 8:44), and the evil one (Matthew 13:19; 1 John 2:13, 14; 3:12; 5:18). With credentials like that, it is surprising that he is so good at winning friends and influencing people.

Satan is crafty (Genesis 3:1). His first question to the woman seemed rather innocent on the surface. "Is it true," he said, "that God has prohibited you from eating of any

14

tree in the garden?" He knew it was, and he wasn't asking for information. How that question came across to Eve depends largely on Satan's inflection. I think that it was dripping with incredulity. "Surely God has not given *you* a prohibition. Don't tell me that your loving Creator has held back something from *you*, of all people?" Satan feigned disbelief. It is ever his purpose to use lying disbelief to plant real disbelief in his victims. He delights in nothing more than in leading us to doubt God.

Satan wanted the woman to look at the tree from the wrong angle. The tree stood, in God's good provision, as a blessing through which a free moral agent could demonstrate his faith relationship to God. But Satan wanted her to view it as an unnecessary, unfair impingement upon her God-given freedom.

One of Eve's problems was that she enjoyed this seemingly enlightened, stimulating, sophisticated, and sympathetic conversation with Satan. Her reply began well. It called attention to the fact that God had provided all that she needed in the other trees of the garden (3:2). There may have been doubt of God's propriety, however, in the latter part of her reply. Her addition of the information that this tree ought not even to be touched may be incidental. Or it may be an indication that she had begun to imitate Satan's incredulity. "Why," she perhaps exclaimed, "we can't even *touch* that tree!"

Something in her reply told Satan that she was ready for the big lie. She began to see the obedience tree as somehow in contradiction to God's love. Satan succeeded in getting her to wonder at the prohibition of the garden rather than to wonder at the provision of the garden. Satan still uses that well-tried tactic. He wants us to look disappointedly at what God asks us to avoid rather than to look thankfully at what He provides, hoping to make us believe that what is withheld is really better for us than what God provides.

God had said that the tree of testing meant death, but Satan flatly contradicted Him, "You surely shall not die!" The bigger the lie, and the more emphatic the conviction with which it is said, the more likely it is to be believed. Satan called God a liar. Since the lie was cast in the realm of

15

the future, Eve had to decide between God and Satan on faith. Should she believe God, who had formed her and given her so much, or should she believe this flashy talker with the dramatic style?

Had Eve been paying attention and using her mind properly at this point, she would have recognized Satan for the liar he is. She would have known that no being, whether bright-shining or slimy-slithering, can call God a liar and be of the truth. Satan still persists in pulling off that deception. How frequently we hear in our day that God's revelation is not true to reality, true to nature, or true to the necessities of our time.

Satan supported his assertion by verbalizing a concept he had previously implied. He made the slanderous claim that God was holding out on man, that God did not really have the best interests of man at heart either in His design of the garden or in His revelation of the fixed truths of the garden.

Lies are always more convincing if supported by half-truths. Satan promised that the woman would be like God, knowing good and evil. She interpreted that promise, as Satan intended, to be a desirable thing. She was to learn, to her sorrow, that it can be a terrible thing. (Satan used here a technique favored by false advertisers ever since. The principle is to advertise your product's defect as a great and beneficial advancement.)

In Genesis 3:22, we hear God saying, "Behold, the man has become like one of Us, knowing good and evil." "Well, what is wrong with that?" we say. "Isn't it desirable to know the difference between good and evil? Doesn't God want us to have discerning ability so that we will identify and shun the evil? Didn't Eve purchase us a valuable gift through her disobedience?"

No, she didn't. We know that Adam and Eve had the moral sensibility we are talking about before the fall. They had enough moral sense for God to appeal to it with his negative commandment concerning the tree. But they did not have *experiential knowledge* of evil. They did not know it by having done it. That was the bitter knowledge they acquired—the carnal knowledge that brings alienation, shame, suffering, and death.

Our sinning parents became like God, knowing good and evil. Just how does God know evil? Certainly He does not know it, as Adam and Eve did, from doing it. Ray Stedman, in his exciting book, *Understanding Man*, wrote that

> God knows evil, not by experiencing because he cannot experience evil, but by relating it to Himself. That which is consistent with His character and His nature is good; that which is inconsistent with it is evil. That which is out of line, out of character with Himself is evil, destructive, and dangerous; but all that is in line with His own nature is good. That is how God 'knows' good and evil. He relates it to Himself.
>
> But God is the only one who can properly do that. God is the only Being in all the universe who has the right to relate all things to Himself. When a creature tries it he gets into trouble. The creatures of God's universe are made to discover the difference between good and evil by relating all to the Being of God, not to themselves. When man ate of the fruit he began to do what God does—to relate everything to himself . . . When man began to think of himself as the center of the universe, he became like God. But it was all a lie. Man is not the center of the universe, and he cannot be.*

Satan continues with this lie. When he finds a good line, he hangs onto it and uses it again and again. He whispers in our ears that what we think is right is all that matters: there are no absolute rights or wrongs, no absolute goods or evils; what we want to do is right, what we don't want to do is wrong.

---

*From Ray Stedman, *Understanding Man,* ©1975. Used by permission of Word Books, Publisher, Waco, Texas.

That Eden testing tree was a place for the opportunity of experientially knowing good or experientially knowing evil. Until the fall, both Adam and Eve experientially knew good. That was in their nature. As they trusted in God and listened to His instructions, *all* was good. It was the *experience* of evil that they were to learn by disobedience. And Satan made that seem good. That is the way he works, not only distorting our very language, but distorting our very good sense as well.

Meanwhile, back at the testing tree. . . . Satan had just told a lie and followed it with a half truth. It was a critical moment. Had Eve slammed the door of her mind in Satan's lying face, a lot of things about human existence would have been different. Instead of recoiling and running, she remained and rationalized. Her senses cooperated with Satan's deception. The tree appealed to her appetite, a God-given thing. She had been designed with the ability to taste and enjoy, to savor and appreciate, to smell and relish. The fruit not only seemed quite edible and delectable to the taste buds, it looked beautiful to the eye as well. Her God-given aesthetic sense, designed by God to make her appreciative of His works of creative genius, became the instrument of her rationalization of evil. Her aspiration for wisdom, a God-given mental faculty, was used by Satan to defeat true wisdom (Genesis 3:6). Satan, of course, did not see fit to remind her that "the fear of the Lord is the beginning of wisdom, and knowledge of the Holy One is understanding" (Proverbs 9:10).

In all of this, Satan capitalized on human drives and appetites to corroborate his deadly deceptions. It is just like the Deceiver to take advantage of human senses to corroborate his nonsense. All Eve's senses were now "go." Her senses of smell and taste said, "Yes!" Her sense of sight said, "By all means!" Her sense of hearing, jammed with Satan's lies and half truths, said, "Seek the forbidden prize. It will do you much good!" How about her sense of touch? "She took from its fruit and ate" (Genesis 3:6).

Something terrible happened here. Eve's sensual desires, her fleshy desires, began to line up on the side of Satan's lie. She began to *want* to believe the lie. In the process of falling in love with the forbidden tree, she was falling in love with

Satan's lie. This pattern of Satan still operates in our world. There are countless people among us who, because of their fleshly desires, desperately want Satan's lies to be true (Romans 1:20-32; 8:5-8). When we begin to *want to believe* what Satan says about sin rather than what God says about it, we are moving dangerously close to the act of disobedience. Have you ever wished that your conscience would allow you to "enjoy" the immorality and sinfulness that others seem to be enjoying? Have you ever wanted to believe that God does not care about your "little human failings," your euphemism for what God calls sin? It is Satan's plan to turn testing into sin by laying hold of our wills and leading us to *want* to believe his lies.

Let us review Satan's tactic in the garden. He planted in Eve's mind the idea that God was somehow unfair in His dealings with her. He lied to her, then worked with her desires to move her to the point where she wanted to exceed the limitation of God. Coupling Eve's physical, sensual, ego-satisfying desires to his audacious blasphemy, Satan carried off his con. He accomplished this by appealing to Eve's "lust of the flesh," "lust of the eyes," and her "boastful pride of life" (1 John 2:16).

While much is said in a few words about how Eve was deceived, very little is said about the process by which Adam joined Eve outside the limitations of God. Men, always looking for a high motive to justify a low act, would like to believe that he crossed over the line to share the fate of the woman he loved. Yet, it seems somehow more casual than that. The Bible says, "And she gave also to her husband with her, and he ate." It sounds as if he thoughtlessly treated the violation of God's revealed will as a matter without greater consequences. It is one of Satan's ploys to make a life-and-death decision appear to be trivial or inconsequential.

While Satan worked directly on Eve, he worked through her to deceive Adam. Once she had sinned, she became a "pusher" for sin. She wanted Adam to join her, and he did. It is true today that the person who gives himself to disobedience to God becomes an advocate for his sinful life-style. There is nothing that bothers the sinner more than for others to reject his rationalizations for his evil conduct. He

19

will seek to infect others with the fatal virus of sin. Our newsstands are filled with the writings of those who would push their degradation on others, presenting it as freedom that expands the mind, spirit, and senses rather than as the deadly enslavement that it is.

Satan became Eve's silent partner, delighted that now she was a willing accomplice in his death-dealing business. Instead of using her relationship with Adam to help him in his relationship with God, Eve became Satan's instrument in Adam's downfall. Instead of using his relationship with her to help her return to a right relationship with God, Adam joined her in sin.

Satan's promises are sometimes partly true. The eyes of Adam and Eve were opened, but not to the anticipated benefits of disobedience. A self-consciousness replaced God-consciousness; they felt guilty and ashamed. They did not like themselves. Like many a sinner since, they initiated a futile cover-up. But God was fooled by neither fig leaves nor buck-passing.

Instead of receiving the eye-opening experience of knowing evil by doing it that Satan promised, Adam and Eve wanted to block God's vision of them (by hiding) and their vision of each other and themselves (by making clothing). They didn't like the look of themselves, they didn't like the look of each other, and they didn't like the look of God. Sin authors self-deception, the deception of others, and the attempted deception of God. Adam and Eve were somewhat successful with the first two, but in the third they were naked failures. "There is no creature hidden from His sight, but all things are open and laid bare to the eyes of Him with whom we have to do" (Hebrews 4:13).

Formerly, the experience of the presence and the words of God in the cool of the evening marked the high point of each day. Now, the man and the woman *dreaded* God. So they attempted to get Him out of their experience by hiding from Him. The yielding of his will to Satan's lies had altered man's thinking about God. Now He was no longer man's loving companion, his partner in creative endeavor, and the provider of man's "good." Rather He was the unwelcome voice of justice and truth, truth that man no longer wanted to hear.

When God asked, "Where are you?", Adam did not reply with a geographic location. He did not say, "Here we are, hiding under the lemon tree." He replied in terms of his inner state. He was afraid. He was ashamed. He was in a state where what he wanted most was to escape from the view of God. Before, God's overview was a desired and comforting thing. Now it was frightening.

Whose fault was this change of relationship, Adam's, Eve's, Satan's, or God's? God asked Adam if he had gone beyond God's limits. His question was one of fact. Adam's reply was one of fault. He did not want to take the full responsibility for his sin. That tendency remains with man. He blames parents, blames society, blames other people, and ultimately blames God for faulty workmanship in his creation. Adam blamed Eve and God ("the *woman* whom *You* gave to me," 3:12); Eve blamed Satan and God ("the serpent, [one of Your creations and Satan's instrument]" 3:13).

It is true that God provided in the garden the point of possible sin. But God had no desire for man to sin. On the contrary, God desired the tree to be a point of firm trust in Him. The tree, from God's point of view, was an encouragement to good, not evil. It was designed to demonstrate man's freely-given obedience to the limits imposed by the wisdom and providence of God.

Satan, however, by lies and distortions, working with the desires of man, turned God's good thing into a vehicle of suffering and death. God provides the point of testing, Satan uses that point as an opportunity to lead us into rebellion against God, and we freely decide whether to believe God or believe Satan. If Satan is rejected, the test or temptation has served an ennobling purpose. James wrote,

"Blessed is a man who perseveres under trial; for once he has been approved, he will receive the crown of life, which the Lord has promised to those who love Him" (James 1:12). He recognizes the beneficial possibilities of testing. But when a man fails in the test, when he succumbs, he is prone to blame it all on God, who put the test there for him. James, however, will have none of that. He nails us with, "Let no one say when he is tempted, 'I am being tempted by God'; for God cannot be tempted by evil, and He Himself does not tempt any one. But each one is tempted when he is carried away and enticed by his own lust. Then when lust has conceived, it gives birth to sin; and when sin is accomplished, it brings forth death. Do not be deceived, my beloved brethren" (James 1:13-16). James is saying, "Don't be deceived, don't be hoodwinked by Satan. The critical vote is in your hand. You can turn testing into a down payment on a crown of life or you can turn it into a down payment on a coffin of death. You do the latter when you believe the Deceiver instead of the Designer, and when you follow your lustful desires instead of God's loving decrees."

But what happens when we "blow it"? What is God's attitude toward us when we stand guilty, trembling, alienated, and exposed, and the flimsy fig leaves of our excuses fail to cover our sin? Does God slap us down and say, "That's all for you!"?

In the curse of the serpent (Genesis 3:14, 15), there is the first hint of God's plan of reconciliation. The seed of the woman, Jesus, would bruise the head of the serpent. But how about God's words to His human creation? The woman would have pain in childbirth and be ruled over by her husband. The man's life would be one of toil, sweat, and death.

Are these things terrible punishments only, or are they something more? Could it be that each of them is a part of God's design for bringing man back to his former relationship with God? Could it be that these things are not curses so much as gracious provision for the good of man? Could it be that woman's pain in childbirth is a test in its own right—a test with great possibilities for the woman to learn to trust God with all her heart—the thing that she had forgotten in the face of Satan's lies and her own desires (1

Timothy 2:15)? Could it be that her submission to her husband is not a bitter yoke for her to carry all her days but rather God's loving provision through which she will learn submissiveness which enables her to gauge her relationship with God? Could it be that man's sweat and his battle with nature for his daily bread are consciously designed by God to school man in the attitude of complete dependence on Him for life itself? Could it be that death itself can be a blessing to man? The very existence of death is a continual prod to man to do righteously. Its mystery forces man to recognize his own limitations. Its overcoming by Jesus is the crowning evidence of God's gracious love for man.

God was thinking of man's good when He sent man out of the garden lest he eat the tree of life and live forever (Genesis 3:22). In his rebellious state, for man to have lived forever would have been tragic. God was looking ahead to the time when death could be viewed not as defeat but victory because of Jesus (1 Corinthians 15:55-58).

Pain ("Why does God permit suffering in the world?"), submission ("Why can't a person do what he pleases?"), toil ("Why is nature so hostile to man?"), and death ("Why did my loved one have to die?") are primary testing points in the lives of each of us. Talk to most people about why they choose not to believe in God and you'll probably find that they choose one of these areas as the ground for not taking the Biblical revelation of the love of God seriously. Yet, each of these areas affords tremendous opportunity for demonstrating trust in God. Each of them is, in a sense, a testing tree. We have opportunity to use them, through Christ, as a means for developing the trusting character God wants of us and for doing what Adam and Eve failed to do, overcoming the deceits of Satan and the rebelliousness of our spirits.

Chapter Two

GOD'S PEOPLE
At the Testing Tree
(Hebrews 11)

The testing tree, the tree of knowledge of good and evil, was the point where Eve faced a critical decision. Should she believe God or Satan? Should she follow her own desires and impulses or listen to God? She and Adam chose the path of disobedience. They disregarded the word of their Creator. They chose to orient their path by poles other than God's clear teaching. We still bear the tragic fall-out of their sin. God, not surprisingly, knew what He was talking about. God's words were true, for He cannot be otherwise (1 John 5:20, Hebrews 6:18). But *man* was other-wise. He chose "wisdom" (Satan's and his own) *other* than God's wisdom.

Since that time, whenever a man or woman faces a moment of deciding whether or not to trust and obey God, he is, as it were, standing at a testing tree. Cain stood at such a testing place when he brought his offering before God (Genesis 4:1-16). When God rejected Cain's sacrifice, Cain had two choices: he could have accepted God's wise counsel. He could have listened to the loving direction God was giving for his future conduct. Instead, he chose the other path. He interpreted God's words only as a prohibition, an unnecessary and uncalled-for intrusion into his personal affairs. Instead

25

of conforming his actions to the revealed will of God, he became angry. God had presumed to intrude with His way when Cain was sure that his own way was entirely good enough. Who was God, anyhow, to tell Cain, independently wise in all such matters, what was the right way to offer a sacrifice? What difference did it make, anyway? We can almost hear his rationalizations as he pouted and fumed (Genesis 4:5).

God, however, pointed the way to happiness and joy. God wanted Cain to replace his contemptuous scowl with a contented smile. God said, "If you do well, will not your countenance be lifted up? And if you do not do well, sin is crouching at the door; and its desire is for you, but you must master it" (Genesis 4:7).

God found Cain's sacrifice unacceptable (Genesis 4:5). This may have been either because of the nature of Cain's sacrifice or because of his attitude in presenting it. At this point, Cain was still standing before the testing tree. He had made a wrong move, but apparently he had not yet sinned. Sin, like a predatory animal stalking him as its prey, was crouching at the door, ready to spring into his life and ravage him.

This moment illustrates graphically the characteristics of temptation. It is that point where two ways are open to us. One way, God's way, makes the trial an occasion for happiness and joy as we experience the blessings of faithfully following God's instructions for life. The other way, Satan's way, opens the door to death-dealing, devouring, devastating, destroying sin (Romans 6:23). Satan beckons us toward that door with deceiving promises. He promises that it is the door to freedom and enrichment. Instead it is the door of death.

God said to Cain, "You must master it," God clearly gave instructions as to how that could be done. "Do well," God said. "Do, trusting me implicitly, what I instruct." But while God gave clear instructions as to the way of victory over sin and Satan, it was Cain who had to make the critical decision. He had to decide whether to master sin or be mastered by it. He could have bolted the door of his heart against it. He could have kept it at bay by praying for God's help. He could have set sin running with its tail between its

26

legs by putting the idea of disobedience from his mind (James 4:7).

Tragically, Cain did not master sin. He opened the door and welcomed it in. Instead of the happy-day face God had promised for obedience, he put on his dooms-day countenance and looked for someone to blame for his problems.

There weren't too many people around at the time to blame. It certainly wasn't his fault that he was feeling so rotten. Cain was sure of that. If God and he were having this feud, it had to be God's fault. Every good rational rationalizer knows that. God was being cruel and unfair to him. No one in the whole world was interested in what he thought of things. Sin had begun to blind his eyes and to corrupt his good sense, as it always does. The problem was within Cain, but he wanted to externalize it. The problem had to be outside somewhere—in God—in the brother. That is the way of sin. When we begin to experience its deadly fallout, we want to find someone else to blame for our awful feelings. We blame God or we blame others. We strike out at God and we strike out at others, for to do one is to do both.

Cain's quarrel was with God; so he killed his brother. We cannot be in rebellion with God and live at peace with our brothers. When we persist in disobedience to God, we adopt a life-style that leads us on a collision course with other people.

Cain expressed his anger with God in his conduct toward his brother. Perhaps he thought, "Abel always walks around with that sickening happy-day smile on his face. He and God are on such good terms that it makes me sick. He's always whistling 'Peace in the Valley' and saying, 'Have a good day!' In this dumb, dreary world, who needs him? And he's on such good terms with God I can hardly take it. If it weren't for him, maybe God would be better satisfied with me."

Sin closed Cain's eyes to love and kinship. He made himself Number One in his concerns. He lost his sense of responsibility for his brother's welfare. His eyes were completely on himself. Let the rest of the world take care of itself. "Am I my brother's keeper?"

Cain, the murderer, was no longer comfortable in the presence of God. Sin created a barrier, as it had for his father and mother. "Cain went out from the presence of the Lord, and settled in the land of Nod, east of Eden" (Genesis 4:16).

Cain failed at the testing tree. At the testing tree, Satan and sin desire us. God desires that we master sin by relying on His truth. God promises the good life if we trust Him. The testing tree is the moment of crisis, the moment where two options are open: the way of submission to sin, and the way to mastery over sin.

The Old Testament is a virtual forest of testing trees. Noah stood at such a testing place when God commanded him to construct the ark. Noah's tree was a tree of triumph. The Scriptures record, "Thus Noah did; according to all that God had commanded him, so he did" (Genesis 6:22). This is the model by which all testing, all temptation, can be turned into triumph. Noah believed that God is and that His revelation of reality is true. He believed and he acted on his belief, knowing that the reward of his obedience (life) was greater than the cost of his obedience (faithfulness). He staked his life on his faith in God, believing that God is and that He is the rewarder of those who seek Him (Hebrews 11:6).

To the Hebrew mind, Abraham was the classic example of victory at the testing trees of life. At the command of God, he set out on a journey, not knowing in the least where he was going (Hebrews 11:8). The testing tree was a trusting tree for Abraham. He believed God (Genesis 15:6). For Abraham, active belief was the essence of righteousness. For Sarah, his wife, the testing tree of bearing a child in her old age was a trusting tree, "since she considered Him faithful who had promised" (Hebrews 11:11).

28

When, in Abraham's old age, God's promise of a son finally came true, God gave him an incomprehensible command. He was to sacrifice that son. The King James Version reads, in Genesis 22:1, "And it came to pass after these things, that God did tempt Abraham." The New American Standard Bible notes that "God tested Abraham." What was the test? It was a situation that involved a command of God, an irrational command from Abraham's point of view. Why should he kill his only son, the one through whom God would logically fulfill His promise to multiply his descendants and bless the earth? Why? Because God said so. That was reason enough. The writer of Hebrews notes,

> By faith Abraham, when he was tested, offered up Isaac; and he who received the promises was offering up his only begotten son; it was he to whom it was said, 'In Isaac your seed shall be called.' He considered that God is able to raise men even from the dead; from which he also received him back as a type (Hebrews 11:17-19).

Abraham did not understand what God had in mind, but he knew that God was able to accomplish what He had promised without any interference from him. The writer of Hebrews says that Abraham offered up Isaac. He did not, in fact, have to do this. But in his mind and in his will and in his intent, he did—reckoning that God's purposes could be accomplished by God in whatever way He chose, whether Abraham understood it all or not. God, Abraham knew, is always true to His word. A secret for turning a testing tree into a trusting tree and into a triumph tree is summed up in Abraham's attitude toward God, "God is able."

Joseph's life was filled with moments of testing. Sold into slavery by his brothers, falsely accused by his master's wife, thrown into a rotting jail, and forgotten by his friend, yet he trusted God in all. When temptation came, Joseph recognized the true issues involved. Sin was an offense against God (Genesis 39:9). Joseph suffered much, but nowhere do we read that his trials tripped him. Satan was never able, so far as we are told, to use his testing as an occasion to turn him against his conscious and constant trust in God (Genesis 45:5, 7, 9). Joseph did not let bitterness drag him down. There was no evil thing that could befall him that God could not turn to good (Genesis 50:20). Even at the moment of death, Joseph was looking forward to the fulfillment of a promise made to Abraham. His dying wish was a statement of unqualified trust in the Word of God (Genesis 50:25; Hebrews 11:22).

Moses stood at the testing tree when he stood before the burning bush in Midian. He well knew how difficult was the task to which God was calling him. He had grown up in Egypt. He knew the power of Pharaoh. He knew the weakness of the descendants of Jacob. What God promised to do was preposterous from any sensible point of view (Exodus 3:20-22). Moses was only one man. He was not a persuasive speaker or a commanding personality. He was being asked to confront a mighty military establishment with nothing more than God's promised miracles. Ultimately, "By faith he left Egypt, not fearing the wrath of the king; for he endured, as seeing Him who is unseen" (Hebrews 11:27).

In the wilderness, the children of Israel learned much about testing. They began by trusting God implicitly as He led them out of Egypt and through the Red Sea (Hebrews 11:29). It was not long, however, before their trust was put to severe test by conditions they found in the wilderness. Their situation required absolute, unquestioned trust in God to look out for their welfare and meet their needs. The wilderness experience for Israel became a forest of testing trees. For forty years, they were schooled in the ways of God and the waywardness of man. It was a period for building trust into the very bones and marrow of God's people.

In the King James Version, we read a rather curious passage about that situation: "Wherefore do ye tempt the Lord?" Moses thunders at the people of Israel (Exodus 17:2). In this study, we have considered God's testing of man, but how is it that man can test God? That seems to be a strange reversal indeed.

Remember that God, with mighty miracles, prepared the way for the exodus from Egypt. He miraculously brought His people through the Red Sea on dry land. He destroyed the army that raced after them. Then in the wilderness, He gave them food. All they had to do was pick it up in the morning. But then, one day, they ran short of water. Despite all that God had provided in the past, they were not sure they could rely on Him for their present and future needs. They grumbled and criticized. They were so angry at *God* for their thirst that they nearly stoned *Moses*. (Shades of Cain!) God might have done all sorts of things in the past, they murmured, and He might promise to do all sorts of things in the future, but where was the water they needed *now*?

The absence of water in the wilderness became a testing tree for Israel, and they made it a testing tree for God. "Why do you test the Lord?" Moses asked (Exodus 17:2). In their minds were other questions. "Is God's wisdom sufficient to meet our needs? Is He really with us? Don't the present circumstances justify doubt? Is the Lord with us or not?" (Exodus 17:7).

This testing tree in the wilderness became, in the minds of Old Testament writers, a classic example of God-forgetfulness.

> How often they rebelled against Him in the wilderness,
> And grieved Him in the desert!
> And again and again they tempted God,
> And pained the Holy One of Israel.
> They did not remember His power,
> The day when He redeemed them from the adversary. . . .
> Yet they tempted and rebelled against the Most High God,
> And did not keep His testimonies,
> But turned back and acted treacherously like their fathers;
> They turned aside like a treacherous bow.
>
> (Psalm 78:40-42, 56, 57).

Earlier in the same Psalm we read,

And in their heart they put God to the test
By asking food according to their desire.
Then they spoke against God;
They said, "Can God prepare a table in the wilderness?"

(Psalm 78:18, 19)

Meribah became proverbial for the place of the hardened heart and the doubting spirit.

Today, if you would hear His voice,
Do not harden your hearts, as at Meribah,
As in the day of Massah in the wilderness;
"When your fathers tested Me,
They tried Me, though they had seen My work."

(Psalm 95:7-9)

And in Psalm 106:13, 14, we also read,

They quickly forgot His works;
They did not wait for His counsel,
But craved intensely in the wilderness,
And tempted God in the desert.

Paul wrote that they craved evil things (1 Corinthians 10:5, 6) during their wilderness experience. Water was certainly not evil, but what they were doing in their obsession for it most certainly was. They spoke against God and against His provision (Numbers 21:5-7).

Israel stumbled again at the testing tree when spies were sent into Canaan. God promised that He certainly would give Canaan into their hands (Numbers 13:2). But when the ten spies reported the strength of the resident forces, the people of Israel doubted God. They feared and rebelled (Numbers 14:9). God was sorely displeased that they had not listened to His voice—that they had put Him to the test (Numbers 14:22).

We see clearly that they were speaking against God

(Numbers 21:5-7) when they should have been listening to God (Numbers 14:22). The writer to the Hebrews had all this in mind when he wrote:

> Therefore, just as the Holy Spirit says,
> "Today if you hear His voice,
> Do not harden your hearts as when they provoked Me,
> As in the day of trial in the wilderness,
> Where your fathers tried Me by testing Me,
> And saw my works for forty years.
> "Therefore I was angry with this generation,
> And said, 'They always go astray in their heart;
> And they did not know my ways. . . .' "
> But encourage one another day after day, as long as it is still called "Today," lest any one of you be hardened by the deceitfulness of sin.
> For we have become partakers of Christ, if we hold fast the beginning of our assurance firm until the end; while it is said,
> "Today if you hear His voice,
> Do not harden your hearts, as when they provoked me. . . ."
> And to whom did He swear that they should not enter His rest, but to those who were disobedient? And so we see that they were not able to enter because of unbelief (Hebrews 3:7-19).

It emerges from these passages that testing God involves doubting God, rebelling against God, grieving God, forgetting God, disobeying God, disbelieving God, ignoring God, hardening the heart against God, following evil cravings, speaking against the ways of God, being ignorant of God's ways, straying from God's path, and being deceived by sin. These behaviors all provoke God. When a person, himself the object of testing, succumbs to the behaviors above, he is testing God. The opposite of putting God to the test is relying unquestioningly on God, believing unfalteringly in God, and trusting implicitly in God. The person who thus responds to God knows that He is capable of doing all that He has said He will do. He knows without question that God is, that He is true, righteous, and loving, that His care is all-encompassing, and that He can be relied on to fulfill all His promises.

It would seem then that man's *failure at the testing place* is the same thing as man's *testing God*. Why is something tested? It is tested to see whether it will do what it is designed for, to see whether it lives up to its promised performance, to see whether it is worth the money that it costs, to see whether it will last. Faith, dependence, trust, and obedience to God absolutely rule out testing as an appropriate thing for man to do to God. Faith means that we do not question that God will do what He says, that He is worth our unquestioning allegiance, and that He will be with us always and in all circumstances. Faith trusts that He will never fail or let us down. Calling upon God to prove himself on our terms, to our satisfaction, is the direct antithesis of faith.

On the other hand, it is appropriate for God to test man. Tests refine a product and improve it. God cannot be improved. Man can, because he is flawed by sin. The tests that come to man are designed for his benefit, not his breakdown (Psalm 7:9; 1 Chronicles 29:17; Psalm 11:5; 139:23, 24; Proverbs 17:3; Jeremiah 20:12).

The sin of putting God to the test is mentioned a number of times in the New Testament as well. In the fifth chapter of Acts, we read of Peter's confrontation with a woman by the name of Sapphira and with her husband Ananias. He said to her, "Why is it that you have agreed together to put the Spirit of the Lord to the test?" That sin was significant enough to bring death to her and her conspiring husband. What had they done? They had opened their hearts to the lies of Satan, just as Eve had. They had listened to him and they had adopted his style, falsehood. They tried to lie to the Holy Spirit and to God (Acts 5:1-11). God was not amused. When they put God to the test, they, in that very act, failed *their* tests by succumbing to Satan. God could not let such a sin pass unpunished in the early church. The very integrity and authority of God were at stake.

When a dispute arose as to whether Jews should be circumcised, some of the Pharisees were determined that it was necessary for the Gentiles to observe the Mosaic law in this matter. Peter, who had received a vision that had sent him to preach to a Gentile soldier, realized that God had broken down the barrier between Jews and Gentiles. He said, "Now therefore why do you put God to the test by placing upon the neck of the disciples a yoke which neither our fathers nor we have been able to bear?" (Acts 15:10). Here again we note that putting God to the test is withstanding His revealed will, failing to implement His commands, and substituting human wisdom for the divine. To put God to the test is to question Him when He should be accepted, to doubt Him when He should be trusted, and to relate things to self when they should be related to the divinely revealed mind of God. Such is emphatically not appropriate behavior toward the almighty, perfect Creator of all that is.

While we have noted that in a number of instances those who tested God were immediately brought to task for their rebellious conduct, it frequently seems that evil people prosper. They seem to escape God's judgment (Malachi 3:15). They are arrogant, wicked, and do everything but serve God (Malachi 3:15, 18). Yet, this ought not to fret us. The righteous will be blessed and God will set things in order in His own good time (Malachi 4).

The New Testament frequently tells us of those who came to test Jesus by asking Him questions. Some came in a genuine spirit. Others came, not out of sincere desire for truth, but out of a desire to ensnare Him (John 8:6). Despite all the signs and wonders He performed in their midst, they would not bring themselves to believe on Him. In an incident recorded in Luke 11:16, for example, Jesus had just brought speech to a man who formerly had been unable to talk. Rather than believing Him for what had just happened, they demanded a sign from Heaven. In this, they were not unlike many of us who want evidence of God other than what He has already so readily supplied. We ask Him to prove himself to us rather than accepting Him on the basis of what He has already done.

There are countless other examples of victory and defeat in moments of testing by Bible people. David was a man who met innumerable crises in a spirit of trust in God. Yet he too succumbed to Satan. He saw the beautiful Bathsheba, the wife of his faithful soldier, and desired her (the lust of the eye and the lust of the flesh). He committed adultery with her, then arranged for the murder of her husband. When confronted with his sin by Nathan, God's prophet, David humbled himself, saying, "I have sinned against the Lord" (2 Samuel 12:13). God forgave him, but his sin led to bitter consequences for him and for others.

Hebrews 11 closes with a breathtaking chronicle of the tests and tribulations of God's people. From the world's point of view their lives were wasted failures, but from God's point of view they were more than conquerors in the testing times. "These people all trusted God and as a result won battles, overthrew kingdoms, ruled their people well, and received what God had promised them . . ." (Hebrews 11:33, TLB*).

---

*TLB is The Living Bible, ©1971 by Tyndale House Publishers, Wheaton, Illinois.

Chapter Three

JESUS
At the Testing Tree
(Luke 4:1-13; Romans 5)

What was Jesus really like? He had a human body with human needs. He had a nature in many ways just like ours. But He was also unlike us. He was God. Partaking of our nature, He experienced temptation. Partaking of God's nature, He overcame every temptation. Since He was God, one might be tempted to think that His temptations were not as real as ours. Yet, our tendency is to cave in to the holds of Satan long before he has applied his full weight to us. Jesus, in contrast, did not give in. He bore all that Satan could bring to bear on Him, yet He was not overcome.

Jesus' human nature was not a masquerade. It was as real as ours is. Jesus, tempted, could have succumbed to sin. Jesus was "tempted in all things as we are, yet without sin" (Hebrews 4:15). That means to me that He was tested where I am—in His pride, in His body with its sex drives, in His deeds and their motives, in His relationships with others. In short, He was tested in all areas of human existence, just as I am. But He was victorious in them all (John 8:46). That's where we differ markedly.

The Bible tells us that since Jesus experienced human testing, He is uniquely qualified to sympathize with our weaknesses and to come to our aid when we are tempted (Hebrews 2:18; 4:15).

Jesus, like us, was tempted and tested throughout His lifetime. While there were many testing trees in the life of Jesus, the gospel biographies give prominence to two. One is in the wilderness at the beginning of His ministry. The other is in the capital city shortly before His crucifixion.

Jesus was a young man in the prime of His life. He was

37

about thirty years old when He left Nazareth and walked toward the place along the Jordan where John was teaching and baptizing. John recognized that Jesus was the Messiah for whom he had been preparing the way. Consequently, John was reluctant to baptize Jesus. But Jesus replied, "Permit it at this time; for in this way it is fitting for us to fulfill all righteousness" (Matthew 3:15). Thus Jesus began His ministry by demonstrating His determination to conform His actions to righteousness, to God's instructions and requirements. There is nothing more pleasing to God than this. God responded to Jesus' obedience. The Holy Spirit descended upon Him and God's voice spoke forth His pleasure in His beloved Son (Matthew 3:13-17). At Jesus'

baptism, He demonstrated obedience and conformity to the will of God, and God acknowledged Jesus' special kinship to the Father with the Holy Spirit.

This Holy Spirit immediately led Jesus to the testing tree. The Spirit "impelled Him to go" (Mark 1:12) into the wilderness to be tempted by Satan. God's Spirit sent Him forth to do combat with the Evil One. That is at least a part of the Spirit's work, to bring to naught the pretentions of the Evil One. That was Jesus' work, to defeat the ruler of this world (1 John 3:8). It was not that Satan came to Jesus and challenged Him, trying to undo the plan of God that was being set in motion through His Son. It was Jesus who went hunting that "devouring lion" (1 Peter 5:8), meeting him in his lying lair, ready to overcome him at the point where he attempts to accomplish his devilish business—the point of testing, the point of temptation. Satan did not drag Jesus into the wilderness to do battle with Him. Jesus went forth with the urging and power of the Holy Spirit directing Him to the point of contest, the testing tree.

Jesus was tempted of Satan throughout the forty-day period in the wilderness (Luke 4:2). He was put to a severe physical and spiritual test. The three temptations mentioned are typical of those that occurred during that forty days of combat at the testing tree. Satan used every physical, psychological, and spiritual appeal he could to defeat God's only Son. Let us look at the temptations, following the order of Luke's account.

The devil said to Jesus, "If You are the Son of God, tell this stone to become bread" (Luke 4:3). Jesus had not eaten throughout the forty days He had been in combat with Satan in the wilderness. Now He was hungry. His physical body was calling for attention. His natural, human appetite was urging Him to supply its needs. Jesus' body was real. It needed to be  supplied with the nutrients of food. The Word was made flesh (John 1:14); God occupied human stuff. It is not surprising that Satan chose Jesus' human appetite as one of his points of attack. Satan had no illusions about who Jesus was. He opened his temptation with, "If You are the Son of God, and I know You are, then just command that stone over there to turn into bread." He seemed to be saying, "You and I both know You have the power to do it, so why don't You? You and I both know You could use a little bread, so why not use a little of Your power to take care of yourself? The benefits of course would be great—Your body would survive. That's important if You are going to be around to fulfill your ministry. And it would probably taste pretty good just now. It wouldn't really cost You anything. What's there to lose? God, after all, gave You that digestive system of yours and its hunger pangs. He created You with that desire to supply Your body's needs. He gave You that stomach, and He surely wouldn't want You to die prematurely here in the wilderness just when You are starting out on Your work. You have the need and You have the power. It is obvious what You should do. Don't sweat it. Look out for yourself. That's what God would really like for You to do. Take care of yourself. Sure, You have God's Spirit, and sure, He says He will provide for You, but where is God now that You really need Him? Why not act independently from Him, just this once?"

This was the testing tree of the physical. Satan had used this same ploy successfully on Eve. She had come to the tree of the knowledge of good and evil. She saw that the tree "was good for food." Now Satan tried the same thing on Jesus, appealing to Him through His appetite. It is the basic satanic appeal to the "lust of the flesh" (1 John 2:16).

But Jesus, unlike Eve, was not fooled. He refused to play Satan's game on Satan's terms. He turned the testing into triumph. His example should instruct us how to turn our own testing into victory. First, He went to the Word of God. He chose to take His stand on the revealed mind of God. He chose to define things, not in terms of human appetites or human needs, but in God's terms. God has revealed that His primary concern, unlike Satan's, is the wholeness of the inner man. The godly man's hunger is not just for bread, it is for something more lasting, more nourishing, more sustaining, the Word of God. Jesus' reply nailed Satan at the tempting tree. "It is written, Man shall not live on bread alone, but on every word that proceeds out of the mouth of God" (Matthew 4:4). Jesus was later to say, "My food is to do the will of Him who sent Me, and to accomplish His work" (John 4:34). Here we see Jesus doing exactly what Adam and Eve had failed to do. He is taking God at His word. He is determined to do nothing that is not the will of God. He will rest His whole being completely on the knowledge and providence of God and will allow neither His human appetites and instincts nor His human wisdom to lead Him outside God's will. Life is more than eating and digesting; it is trusting the whole self to God.

The two combatants were transported then to a high mountain where Satan, in a moment of time, spread out before them all the kingdoms of the world with all their splendor, wealth, and glory. It must have been a breath-taking view. The wealth, power, and glory of all nations then and in the future glittered before them. It was a vision calculated to excite the mind. Power and glory—the goals that have led countless people to wreak havoc on the earth—were there for the taking.

Satan twisted the truth, as is his wont, as he gave his pitch. The realms of power and glory certainly are his sphere of activity. They represent the material world, which he pushes as the "only world." It is enticing stuff indeed. Unless we stay with God's teaching on the relative importance of the material and the spiritual, we are easily led to believe that we ought to devote ourselves entirely to the attainment of the material. But Satan has not created the material. God did that, and He made it good. It was intended to be good for man. But Satan, by encouraging man to look at the material as the beginning and end of life, had worked another one of his lies. Satan had succeeded very well with his plan of getting man to worship the created thing rather than the Creator (Romans 1:25). Now he was employing one of his tried and true (Or should we say tested and assuredly false?) deceptions on Jesus.

Satan claimed authority over the kingdoms of the earth, but that too was not entirely true. His rule, like everything else about him, is an illusion. God is ultimately in complete control of the universe (1 Chronicles 29:12). Further, Satan had a little price tag attached to the gift he neither fully owned nor could truly give. All he wanted was that Jesus fall down and worship him. To worship Satan would be to acknowledge Satan's right  to obedience, to sovereign rule in His life. It would be sub-version of complete loyalty to the One who must be the object of total loyalty.

For Jesus, the temptation was to assume kingship in this world by a way other than the cross. It was to deviate from God's plan of the perfect sacrifice of God's perfect Son. It was a temptation to step outside God's parameters and to seek a human rather than a divine goal by a disobedient rather than divine way.

This temptation seems to involve the "lust of the eye" (1 John 2:16). Man's desires, man's covetous spirit, reaches out for those forbidden things that his eye sees or his mind's eye imagines. Eve saw a fruit that "was a delight to the eyes" (Genesis 3:6). Her eyes saw the tempting reward, but they did not see the tragic results of disobedience to God. Satan in Eden had used her desires to blind her to the realities of the unseen world. He tried the same thing with Jesus, but with Him, Satan failed.

Jesus once again went to the revealed Word of God for His reply. It is that Word that must always be the standard of conduct. "It is written." It is written in God-given Scripture. God's will is recorded there for all to see and know. "You shall worship the Lord your God and serve Him only." No one but God is worthy of worship. God's commands and statutes make it clear that His people must love God with all their heart and soul and might (Deuteronomy 6:5). Moses said,

> You shall fear only the Lord our God; and you shall worship Him, and swear by His name. . . . You shall not put the Lord your God to the test, as you tested Him at Massah. You should diligently keep the commandments of the Lord your God, and His testimonies and His statutes which he commanded you.
>
> (Deuteronomy 6:13-17)

This constituted the first and great commandment of the law (Matthew 22:36-38).

Jesus was not tricked by Satan's pretensions. It is always Satan's desire to divert worship and service from God to himself.

Then Jesus and Satan were transported to a high place in the temple. There Satan himself appealed to Scripture to test Jesus. This too is Satan's way, to use misquoted Scripture against itself. He was trying to use God's Word against God. He said, "If You are the Son of God, cast Yourself down from here; for it is written, 'He will give His angels charge concerning You to guard You,' and, 'On their hands they will bear You up, lest You strike Your foot against a stone' " (Luke 4:9-11). How diabolical of Satan—to use God's revelation as a means of tempting Jesus to do other than God's will! Satan quoted from Psalm 91, a beautiful psalm that emphasizes the security of the one who trusts in the Lord. There the benefits of dwelling in the shelter of the Most High and abiding in the shadow of the Almighty are described. To such a one God promises to "give His angels charge concerning you, to guard you in all your ways. They will bear you up in their hands, lest you strike your foot against a stone." It is a wonderful promise of protection and defense.

Satan's deceit lay in the fact that he was inviting Jesus to step outside the shelter and shadow of God. He was inviting Him to seek a way to Messiahship outside the path that God had ordained. Satan was urging Jesus to do things other than in God's way. He was urging Him to take things into His own hands rather than waiting on the provision of God to make His Messiahship known.

Jesus recognized that Satan's urging was not, as Satan wanted it to appear, an act of reliance on the promises of God. Rather it was putting God to the test. Jesus responded, "It is said, 'You shall not put the Lord your God to the test' " (Luke 4:12; cf. Deuteronomy 6:16). In our chapter, "God's People at the Testing Tree," we discussed what that involved. Man is to trust God, not test Him. The people of Israel tested God when they were unwilling to allow Him to act in His way, in His time. Testing God involves doubting God and His commandments, forgetting God, following human inclinations rather than His revelations, ignoring God's ways, and disbelieving God's words. Jesus was determined that He would follow God's leading wholly and completely. The way to Messiahship would be the way of the cross, not the way of dramatic daring.

This test is similar to Satan's enticement of Eve. The fruit, Eve believed, was desirable "to make one wise" (Genesis 3:6). Wisdom is a good thing and ought to be sought, just as God's protection is good and ought to be sought. But wisdom is to be found in heeding the commands of God, not in violating them. God's protection also is to be found in heeding the commands of God, not in violating them. God's protection also is to be found in heeding God's plan, not in abandoning it. Satan, the deceiver, was extremely subtle here. What he urged, on the surface, seemed desirable—complete trust in God to protect and supply, casting one's fate completely on the promise of God to save. But Satan had twisted things. What was a good situation in the right context, under the protection, shadow, and shelter of God, was evil when it was pursued as a substitute for simple reliance on God.

It was an invitation to move independently, outside of God's plan. This temptation appealed to what John calls "the boastful pride of life" (1 John 2:16). This is man's desire to act independently from God, to construct his own course of action, apart from God's way. Satan crushes many at this testing tree. He tempts us to do good things (trust in God to save and protect) in the wrong way (putting God to the test) for the right purpose (to gain recognition for God) in the wrong way (by averting God's plan).

 Satan was utterly defeated in each of his attempts to turn testing into sin. He used all the tricks in his bag of illusions, his every persuasive appeal, his every twisted truth and insidious lie. Jesus was not conned. He knew God's will so thoroughly, He was determined to do it so resolutely, He relied upon God's Word so faithfully, that Satan could not deceive Him. Finally, defeated, Satan departed from Jesus. He had been valiantly resisted and now he could do nothing but flee (James 4:7).

But Satan did not give up. He was to return again and again to work with the testing of Jesus' life in an attempt to turn that testing into sin rather than strength. Satan left Jesus for a time, until another opportune moment came (Luke 4:13). Satan is persistent. He was defeated at every turn by Jesus, yet he kept at his death-dealing work. He would continue until he was finally put in his place by Jesus (Hebrews 2:14, 15).

This cosmic struggle was not going unnoticed by God. He did not intervene to lessen the weight of the temptations for Jesus. Yet, when Jesus had stood the tests, God sent His messengers to minister to Him (Matthew 4:11). God lovingly provided what He needed. Having been tested and having been found faithful, He was now ready to teach and preach. He returned to Galilee in the power of the Spirit (Luke 4:14).

Our attention now goes from this testing tree at the beginning of the ministry of Jesus to one near the end of His earthly life. Jesus had just observed the Passover meal with His disciples. Then they had sung a hymn together and had gone out to a garden on the lower slope of the Mount of Olives. There, in Gethsemane, He prayed with His disciples. He urged His disciples to pray, especially that they would not enter into temptation, trial, or testing (Luke 22:40). Jesus himself "was deeply grieved, to the point of death" (Matthew 26:38). He prostrated himself on the ground and prayed, "My Father, if it is possible, let this cup pass from Me; yet not as I will, but as Thou wilt." Three times He prayed these words. Two times He urged His sleeping disciples to be alert and to pray that they not be led into defeat in the testing that was to come (Matthew 26:36-44). Jesus was determined to drink the cup of suffering that lay ahead. The cross was the great testing tree. There He expressed His complete submission to the will of God. The night hours leading up to His arrest were well suited for the work of Satan. He wanted nothing more than to turn Jesus' testing into disobedience and betrayal of God. Satan would soon succeed in getting Peter to do the right thing (stay close to Jesus) in the wrong way (by denying Him). Satan had begged earnestly to be able to put Peter to the test that night (Luke 22:31). Jesus, who knew that Peter would buckle in the test, prayed that his faith would survive and that Peter would be able to strengthen the other disciples (Luke 22:32).

Jesus was human. He knew that the way of the cross was one of physical pain and anguish. Yet Satan was not able to get a sin-hold on Jesus through His humanity. His whole being cried out to God, "Nevertheless, not what I want but what You want" (Luke 22:42).

45

The cross was a testing tree for Jesus, and it is a testing tree for us, too. Satan would like us to think that it is foolishness (1 Corinthians 1:18). At the foot of the cross, each of us must decide whether or not to believe God and accept what He has provided for us through Jesus, or turn away to our own desires and ambitions. Satan's defeat was sealed at the cross, but he still persists in his dying cause.

Jesus nailed to the Calvary testing tree the decrees that were against us. His victory was not a victory for himself, but for all of us who participate in His death, burial, and resurrection through faith, trust, and obedience to God. Paul wrote to the Colossians,

> And when you were dead in your transgressions and the uncircumcision of your flesh, He made you alive together with Him, having forgiven us all our transgressions, having cancelled out the certificate of debt consisting of decrees against us and which was hostile to us; and He has taken it out of the way, having nailed it to the cross. When He had disarmed the rulers and authorities, He made public display of them, having triumphed over them through Him.
>
> (Colossians 2:13-15)

The New English Bible* states verse 15 thus: "On that cross he discarded the cosmic powers and authorities like a garment; he made a public spectacle of them and led them as captives in his triumphal procession."

In His death, as in His life, Jesus was obedient to God. "And being found in appearance as a man, He humbled Himself by becoming obedient to the point of death, even death on a cross" (Philippians 2:8). That victory was made complete with Jesus' resurrection and enthronement at the right hand of God.

> Therefore also God highly exalted Him, and bestowed on Him the name which is above every name, that at the name of Jesus every knee should bow, of those who are in heaven, and on earth, and under the earth, and that every tongue should confess that Jesus Christ is Lord, to the glory of God the Father.
>
> (Philippians 2:9-11)

---

*The New English Bible (NEB) ©1961, 1970, The Delegates of the Oxford University Press and the Snydics of the Cambridge University Press.

What a resounding victory over Satan! And what far-reaching implications for the descendants of fallen Adam and Eve. Our ancestors' sin brought estrangement and alienation into the world as a fact of life. Jesus' shed blood reversed the situation entirely.

Through Him, God chose to reconcile the whole universe to himself, making peace through the shedding of His blood upon the cross—to reconcile all things, whether on earth or in Heaven, through Him alone.

> Although you were formerly alienated and hostile in mind, engaged in evil deeds, yet He has now reconciled you in His fleshly body through death, in order to present you before Him holy and blameless and beyond reproach—if indeed you continue in the faith firmly established and steadfast, and not moved away from the hope of the gospel that you have heard, which was proclaimed in all creation under heaven.
>
> (Colossians 1:21-23)

Jesus rescued us from Satan's dungeon and returned us once again to safety in His Father's kingdom. "He delivered us from the domain of His beloved Son, in whom we have redemption, the forgiveness of sins (Colossians 1:13, 14). Now, through Jesus, man can have peace with God (Colossians 1:20).

The obedience of Jesus on the cross reversed the consequences of man's disobedience in Eden. Thus Jesus crushed the serpent's head (Genesis 3:15).

> So then as through one transgression there resulted condemnation to all men, even so through one act of righteousness there resulted justification of life to all men. For as through one man's disobedience the many were made sinners, even so through the obedience of the One the many will be made righteous.
>
> (Romans 5:18, 19)

Jesus turned testing into victory. Never in the process of living or dying did temptation become sin for Him. He "committed no sin, nor was any deceit found in His mouth" (1 Peter 2:22). Suffering on our behalf, He set an example of faithful suffering to be followed in our own trials (1 Peter 2:21).

Chapter Four

THREE

At the Testing Tree:
God's Three-fold Defense Against Temptation
(1 John 1-3; James 4; Ephesians 4, 5; Romans 5, 8;
Colossians 1; Titus 3; 1 Peter 1; 1 Thessalonians 3)

Our studies have scarcely touched the edge of the forest of Biblical testing trees. We want to consider a number of other Scriptures that provide wayposts for our path, guiding us lest we become lost in the high timber of temptation.

The examples that we have studied have shown us that testing can be beneficial as well as destructive. God allows testing in our lives so that we can develop strong inner character (Romans 5:3-5). We have seen in 1 John 2:16 that Satan attempts, at the time of testing, to entice us into rebellion against God by capitalizing on our love for the world (lust of the flesh) and the things of the world (lust of the eyes). Two verses before this, John writes, "I have written to you, young men, because you are *strong,* and *the word of God abides in you,* and you have *overcome the evil one.*" We see, then, that the secret of overcoming the evil one at the testing trees of life is *strength in the Lord* and *the power of His might* (Ephesians 6:10). That strength is related to the Word of God that abides in us. We must make this Word of God a living presence in our conscious and unconscious. It must be engraved upon our hearts (Deuteronomy 11:18; Psalm 119:11; Colossians 3:16). Our goal is not mere intellectual knowledge of God's Word; it is living in such a way as to make God's Word an activating and regulating principle in the whole of our lives (Colossians 1:9-14).

Satan, however, seeks to turn testing trees into sin

49

stumps for stumbling. His strategy is to use man's love for the world and the things in the world to untrack him from simple obedience to God.

He attempts to accomplish this by capitalizing on the *lust of the flesh,* the *lust of the eyes,* and the *boastful pride of life* (1 John 2:16). These three constitute the major components of the "love of the world." They are therefore the three fronts at which our spiritual warfare must be fought. At these three strategic areas, Satan makes his strongest attack. At these three vulnerable areas, we must be victorious if we are to stand against him.

By now, this tragic triad—the lust of the flesh, the lust of the eyes, and the boastful pride of life—has become an old familiar friend, though "friend" seems hardly the word. We saw clearly that Satan used precisely these three points of attack to his advantage in his successful deception of Eve (Genesis 3:6). It was at these three points also that Satan made his unsuccessful assault on Jesus (Luke 4:1-13). They are, as well, the siege points in Satan's strategy for overcoming us.

The *lust of the flesh,* as we noted earlier, corresponds with Eve's observation that the fruit in Eden was "good for food." It is the area of our appetites. The *lust of the eyes* corresponds with Eve's observation that the fruit was "a delight to the eyes." It is the area of our desire to *have* what the eyes see, the material things of this world. The *boastful pride of life* corresponds with Eve's observation that the tree was "desirable to make one wise." It refers to our desire for autonomy, the desire to follow our own ways apart from

50

God's. In a very real way, the first two are evidences of the existence of the third. The boastful pride of life describes our position in relation to God when we follow the two lusts, the lust of the flesh (the love of the world) and the lust of the eyes (the love of the things of the world).

The Terrible Triad

Writing to the Thessalonians concerning their battle with Satan on the fronts of the terrible triad, Paul gave instructions as to how the Christian "ought to walk and please God."

> For this is the will of God, your sanctification; that is, that you abstain from sexual immorality [*lust of the flesh*]; that each of you know how to possess his own vessel in sanctification and honor, not in lustful passion [*lust of the flesh*], like the Gentiles who do not know God; and that no man transgress and defraud his brother in the matter [*lust of eyes, lust of flesh*] because the Lord is the avenger in all these things, just as we also told you before and solemnly warned you. For God has not called us for the purpose of impurity, but in sanctification [*counter to boastful pride of life*].
>
> (1 Thessalonians 4:3-7)

Sanctification, it would seem, is opposed to the boastful pride of life, in that we are set aside to God, not standing aside from God to ourselves. The Holy Spirit stands with us in this conflict. To reject His aid is to reject God (1 Thessalonians 4:8). Paul's defenses against Satan's attack include love (1 Thessalonians 4:9, 10), quiet life (4:11), hard work (4:11), and self-provision (4:12).

In order to stand against Satan, we must "put on the Lord Jesus Christ" and abandon our reliance on our own physical desires, our own material possessions, and our own independent, prideful spirit. It is clear that we are no match for Satan on our own. He is a spiritual being of great cunning. We are wrestling with principalities and powers and the rulers in high places (Ephesians 6:12). We can, however, overwhelmingly conquer through Christ (Romans 8:37). Without Christ in us, we have no hope of standing with confidence and joy in the trials of living. Our own efforts cannot withstand Satan's power, but Jesus, who overcame Satan when He was in human form, can overcome Satan now in us. John wrote, "We know that no child of God is a sinner; it is the Son of God who keeps him safe, and the evil one cannot touch him" (1 John 5:18 NEB).

When he gives his life to Jesus, the believer enters into a special alliance with God, who seals him off from Satan's power by the Holy Spirit (Ephesians 4:30). Together, he and God's Spirit within him prepare for the struggle, putting away all bitterness and wrath and anger and clamor and slander and malice—*lust of the flesh, lust of the eyes, pride of life*—and erecting strong barriers against Satan through tenderness—*defense against Satan's attack through the lust of flesh and the lust of the eyes*—and forgiveness—*defense against Satan's attack through pride of life* (Ephesians 4:31, 32).

Satan meets us at the testing trees of our lives and attempts to get us to step outside God's revealed will. His ultimate aim is to subvert us into violation of the "Godlines" of human conduct. Satan's will is nothing less than making us captives of sin and hostages of death (Romans 6:23).

The Scriptures reveal, however, that God has provided strong bulwarks to block Satan at each attack point through which he seeks to overcome and enslave us. At the three points of battle, the terrible triad, there are three strong, God-provided defenses. We might term them the triumphant triad. Paul identified them when he wrote to the Thessalonians: "But since we are of the day, let us be sober, having put on the breastplate of *faith* and *love*, and as a helmet, the *hope* of salvation" (1 Thessalonians 5:8). Faith, love, hope—these three Paul identified as prime defensive armor against subversion by the evil one.

THE TRIUMPHANT TRIAD!

Love, faith, and hope, Christ Jesus, God, the Holy Spirit, and the Word of God are all inextricably linked in Scripture. Paul wrote, "For we through the *Spirit,* by *faith,* are waiting for the *hope* of righteousness. For in *Christ Jesus* neither circumcision nor uncircumcision means anything, but *faith* working through *love*" (Galatians 5:5, 6). He wrote also to Timothy,

> For this reason I also suffer these things, but I am not ashamed; for I know whom I have believed [*faith*] and I am convinced that He is able [*hope*] to guard [*protect*] what I have entrusted to Him [*hope*] until that day. Retain the *standard of sound words* which you have heard from me [Word of God], in the *faith* and *love* which are in *Christ Jesus. Guard, through the Holy Spirit* who dwells in us, the treasure which has been entrusted to you.
> (2 Timothy 1:12-14)

Through love, faith, and hope we enter into sacred alliance with Christ, God, and the Spirit. They take their abode in us, and they provide for our security. Love, faith, and hope all are our responses to the Godhead. At the same time, they can be viewed as gifts of the Godhead to us. As we accept God's love, as we entrust ourselves to Him, and as we rest on His promises, we have God's power working within us, strengthening us in the three areas of battle. God reinforces us with His invincible power, enabling us to "do exceeding abundantly beyond all that we ask or think, according to the power that works within us" (Ephesians 3:20). We conquer not in our strength at all, but in the divine strength in us. We rest secure in God's promise that He makes all things "work together for good [*hope*] to those who *love* God, to those who are called according to His purpose [*faith*]" (Romans 8:28). And we know that if God is for us, no one, whether in the physical world or in the spiritual world, can successfully oppose us (Romans 8:31).

It may be possible that there is a sequential relationship among the elements of our triumphant triad, love leading to faith leading to hope. James suggests a sequential relationship for their counterparts, lust leading to sin leading to death (James 1:14, 15). The bastion against lust is love, rooted in the provision of God. The bastion against sin is faith, rooted in the person of God. The bastion against death is hope, rooted in the promises of God.

Love

Love is the bulwark against Satan's attack through the lust of the flesh. Love, first of all, is directed toward God. It is then expressed by God through us to others (Matthew 22: 35-40). Paul wrote to the Galatians, "For you were called to freedom, brethren; only do not turn your freedom into an opportunity for the flesh, but through love serve one another" (Galatians 5:13). The love of God in us is a powerful defense. Love covers a multitude of sins (1 Peter 4:8). It controls us, for through Christ's death and resurrection it is possible for us to stand on the battlements in new strength, relying on God to shore up our pitiful defensive elements within us so that we are able to withstand (Ephesians 6:11).

Paul clearly saw love as a bastion against Satan as he wrote,

> Who shall separate us from the love of Christ? Shall tribulation, or distress, or persecution, or famine, or nakedness, or peril, or sword [testing trees all]? Just as it is written, "For thy sake we are being put to death all day long; we were considered as sheep to be slaughtered." But in all these things *we overwhelmingly conquer through Him who loved us.* For I am convinced that neither death, nor life, nor angels, nor principalities, nor things present, nor things to come, nor powers, nor height, nor depth, nor any other created thing, shall be able to separate us from the love of God, which is in Christ Jesus our Lord.
>
> (Romans 8:35-39)

Faith

Faith would seem to be a bastion to stand in the way of Satan's attack by way of the lust of the eyes. We have defined the lust of the eyes as our desire for worldly, material things. It is that inner drive that makes us think that we can independently provide the necessities to be content, and that we can bring happiness to others merely by amassing the things that the eye can see. Satan seeks to lead us into an idolatry of possessions that ultimately possess us (1 Timothy 6:17-19).

When, in 1 Timothy 6:19, Paul speaks of those who "take hold of that which is life indeed," he is talking about faith. Faith means taking hold—taking hold of the reality of the unseen spiritual world, taking hold of Jesus, who is Lord and Savior, taking hold of the reality and provision of God. It constitutes the essence of life and reality.

The writer to the Hebrews defined faith, in part, as "the conviction of things not seen" (Hebrews 11:1). The lust of the eyes concentrates on the seen, but faith concentrates on the unseen. Righteousness, godliness, faith, love, and perseverance are unseen assets of inestimable value. In contrast, the material things of this world upon which Satan

55

hopes we will waste ourselves are conducive only to our ruin and destruction.

God is unseen. Faith builds on the spiritual reality that this unseen God really is, and that He is the rewarder (hope) of those who diligently seek Him (Hebrews 11:6). The proper relationship of man to this invisible God is one that honors God and happily seeks citizenship in God's eternal domain (1 Timothy 6:16).

The desire for material security is potent. It is the cause of all sorts of headache, strife, and crime, as our newspapers, TV screens, and inner sensibilities bear witness. Feuds and struggles are not just conflicts that occur between human beings. They are the outward symptoms of inner passions raging within the hearts of individuals.

Peter spoke of Satan as a roaring lion whom we must resist *"firm in [our] faith"* (1 Peter 5:8, 9). Trials and tribulations test our faith, James noted, but they also produce the patience we need if we are to stand resolutely with God (James 1:2-4). It is by faith that the Christian stands (2 Corinthians 1:24). Departure from faith is falling captive to Satan (Hebrews 10:38, 39). Paul urged diligence on the battleground of faith, saying, "Be on the alert, stand firm in the faith, act like men, be strong" (1 Corinthians 16:13).

Faith gives us access to God's grace and to Christ's peace and joy. Paul wrote to the Romans,

> Therefore having been justified by *faith* we have *peace* with God through our Lord Jesus Christ, through whom also we have obtained our introduction by *faith* into this *grace* in which we stand; and we exult in *hope* of the glory of God. And not only this, but we also exult in our tribulations, knowing that tribulation brings about perseverance.
>
> (Romans 5:1-3)

Belief in God can lead to suffering (Philippians 1:29; 2 Timothy 1:12; Hebrews 11), but for the just, belief is the mainspring of life. John wrote, "For whatever is born of God overcomes the world; and this is the victory that has overcome the world—our *faith*. And who is the one who overcomes the world, but *he who believes that Jesus is the Son of God*?" (1 John 5:4, 5). Faith, clearly, is a powerful overcomer of Satan's attack.

Hope

Faith is closely related to hope, for faith is "the assurance of things hoped for" (Hebrews 11:1). It involves confidence in God, who, because of His great love for us, provides for our needs—both physical and spiritual—in this life and in the world to come. Hope is faith looking to the future. Paul urged the Colossians to "continue in the *faith* firmly established and steadfast, and not moved away from the *hope* of the gospel that you have heard" (Colossians 1:23).

Hope is the fortification of God standing against Satan's attack on us through the boastful pride of life. Godly hope *relies on God* to provide in the future as He has in the past. It rests on the authority, power, and wisdom of God, not on anything of ourselves. Hope remembers the works of God in the past and puts confidence in the promises of God for the future (Psalm 78:7).

Hope is a cause for rejoicing that is closely linked to perseverance in tribulation (Romans 12:12). It is the end product of a process that leads from tribulation to perseverance, to proven character, to hope (Romans 5:2-4). The Word of God, the sacred Scripture, is a source of our hope, "For whatever was written in earlier times was written for our instruction, that through perseverance and the encouragement of the Scriptures we might have hope" (Romans 15:4). We should note carefully that hope is linked closely with *perseverance and steadfastness* (Romans 8:24, 25; 1 Thessalonians 1:3) and *purity* (1 John 3:3, 4).

Hope is joyful and peaceful. It relies completely on God's revelation of himself through His past actions as is recorded in the Scripture and His revelation of himself in Jesus. Hope, like faith and love, is a product of the Holy Spirit's activity in us. Paul wrote, "Now may the God of *hope* fill you with all *joy* and *peace* in *believing,* that you may abound in *hope* by the power of the *Holy Spirit*" (Romans 15:13). We lay hold of hope as we give ourselves in faith to Jesus. Hope becomes an anchor of the soul, secure, safe, and steadfast. By hope we enter with Jesus into the Holy of Holies of Almighty God, following Jesus, our great high priest (Hebrews 6:18-20).

Christ in the Christian is his hope of glory (Colossians 1:27; 1 Timothy 1:1). The resurrection of Jesus gives us living hope of an imperishable inheritance reserved in Heaven for us (1 Peter 1:3-5). Jesus' resurrection from the dead and His glory with God make it possible for the believer's faith and hope to be in God. Hope is linked closely with love, faith, and the Word of God. Hope must lead to purification. Lawlessness, stepping outside the bounds of God, and relying on our own proud independent spirit for direction, must be done away.

The Sacred Alliance

We know the will of God and abide in Him through His Word. His Spirit unites with us and works within us to strengthen and empower us to fight the advances of the evil one. Our defense is a combination of our response to God and His resources in us. Paul wrote, "Work out your salvation with fear and trembling; for it is God who is at work in you, both to will and to work for His good pleasure" (Philippians 2:12, 13). The first part of the passage underscores our participation and efforts, the second part emphasizes God's enabling presence, which helps us to will what is right and do what is right, two actions we find exceptionally difficult on our own. With God on our side, we are not vulnerable. "The Lord is faithful, and He will strengthen and protect you from the evil one" (2 Thessalonians 3:3). God's part of the alliance may properly be called grace, for it is contributed, not because of our goodness, but because of God's love and concern.

Faith, hope, and love are all grounded in Jesus (faith), His sacrifice (love), and His resurrection (hope). This, finally, is the essence of the gospel, the good news of victory (1 Corinthians 15:1-4). It is Jesus who abolished death and brought life and immortality through the gospel (2 Timothy 1:10).

We must clearly understand that only in Christ are we peacefully within the protective perimeter of God and the Holy Spirit (Colossians 1:19-23). If we are to know our strength against the Deceiver, then we must examine our love, our faith, and our hope. If they are weak, we tie God's hands to defend us. During our afflictions and our trials we must sink our roots ever more deeply into God's strength.

We conclude, then, that we are kept safe from Satan on the three fronts of his attack by faith, hope, and love. All three are intimately related to the revealed Word of God and to the incarnate Word of God, Jesus. All can be strengthened by trials and tribulations. All are the gifts of God and at the same time our gifts to God. Their basic strength is not in our input, but in God's output for our protection.

Faith, hope, and love are the gates by which we first come to God. They are likewise the gates through which we return to God after we sin. Still further, they are the strong gates that protect us from Satan's attack.

The Defense of My Life

Perhaps we can illustrate the way the defenses of God work by visualizing a castle consisting of interlocking

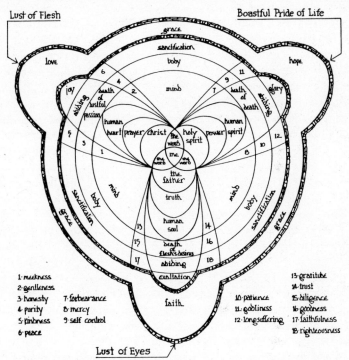

1. meekness
2. gentleness
3. honesty
4. purity
5. kindness
6. peace
7. forbearance
8. mercy
9. self control
10. patience
11. godliness
12. long suffering
13. gratitude
14. trust
15. diligence
16. goodness
17. faithfulness
18. righteousness

walls, battlements, bastions, and gates. The castle has outer walls, inner walls, and a citadel or keep in the center. The diagram above illustrates my safe position in the central keep, where I am surrounded by the strength of God, Christ, and the Holy Spirit. I am in them and they are in me.

They are separate but one with each other and with me. This inner being may be described as the mind, consisting of the human heart, human spirit, and human soul. "Mind" is frequently used in Scripture to describe the complete inner man (Romans 12:2). This inner man, in unity with God, Christ, and the Holy Spirit through the Word of God, is strengthened with power through the Spirit, with prayer in the name of Christ, and with truth through the revelation of God. The body represents the outer man. This outer man, with his physical desires, is frequently the target of Satan. But true love means the death of lustful passion, whole-hearted faith means the death of the flesh's desires for material things, and hope means the death of death through the resurrection of Christ.

When our whole being—body and mind—are right with God, then we can be said to be sanctified. We are abiding in God and He is abiding in us. We are separated, walled in from the things of the world, set apart within the defensive perimeter of God. Our defense is not of our construction. It is the provision of God, the work of His *grace*. I am strong only because He is strong, because He includes me in His defensive plan, because He is my ally. My realization of God's grace leads to exaltation, joy, and glory. Faith, hope, and love are the outer battlements, strengthened from within by the multiple defenses of God. They have been erected by God to defend me at the places of my weakness. They provide extra strength at the places of Satan's attack.

The numbered words describe characteristics of the Christian whose mind and body are sanctified and whose whole self is shielded by the grace of God. On the battlement of love, waving like banners, are meekness, gentleness, honesty, purity, kindness, and peace. On the battlement of hope can be seen the banners of forbearance, mercy, self-control, patience, godliness, and long-suffering. And from the mastheads on the battlement of faith fly the banners of gratitude, trust, diligence, goodness, faithfulness, and righteousness.

"The Lord is the defense of my life; whom shall I dread?" (Psalm 27:1).

Chapter Five

VICTORY
At the Testing Tree
(Ephesians 6; 1 John 4, 5; Hebrews 6)

We are sometimes like toddling children whose parents have put a folding wooden barrier at the top of the stairway lest we tumble down the stairs  and hurt our independent little heads. To us toddlers, that barrier represents a limitation to our world. We toddle up to it and shake it and try to devise ways to get out of the area that has been made safe for us by our parents. We see the barrier as an unwanted restriction, but our loving parents know that it is a necessity for our safety. They are not keeping us from something that is good for us. They know our nature and our needs better than we do. They are keeping us from something that will harm us.

It is so with the will of God. God's will offers great freedom, but it also contains certain restrictions to prevent our harming ourselves. God knows our nature—He created us in His own image. And He knows it is best for us to conform to the image of His Son (Romans 8:28, 29). That is the reason He prohibits whatever is opposed to that image.

Satan urges us to pout at the restrictions of God and to struggle to go beyond His safety barriers, His commandments.

Satan promises us that his way is better than God's. He

urges us to take matters into our own hands. He appeals to our egotistic, prideful desire to be the master. Like the toddler, we act as if we can take care of ourselves. Our will and self-centeredness impel us to disregard God. In the process we make *ourselves*, not God and truth, the standard for judgment of what is desirable.

Satan wants us to look at the wrong things. He wants us to be like the toddler, who forgets the playroom with all its provisions for his benefit and concentrates all his attention on the barrier at the top of the stairs. We are excited to spend our days ignoring our gifts and wanting other ones.

Satan attempts to use our discouragements, our physical limitation, our trials, and our disappointments to make us doubt God's existence and His gracious love-provision. Satan knows that when we doubt God, when we depart from the strength and protection of His Spirit, and when we look to ourselves for reality, then we are ripe for the "wasting" of Satan.

As we read the Old Testament, we discover that Israel failed as her people came to crave evil things, as they began to trust in things of their own imagination and fabrication, as they gave way to their fleshly appetites, and as they came to question God's will (1 Corinthians 10:1-12). These things happened as "examples for us, that we should not crave evil things, as they also craved" (1 Corinthians 10:6) and fall into sin (1 Corinthians 10:12).

The unspiritual human will is weak and treacherous. Paul visualized this graphically when we wrote,

> For I know that nothing good dwells in me, that is, in my flesh; for the wishing is present in me, but the doing of the good is not. For the good that I wish, I do not do; but I practice the very evil that I do not wish. But if I am doing the very thing I do not wish, I am no longer the one doing it, but sin which dwells in me. I find then the principle that evil is present in me, the one who wishes to do good. For I joyfully concur with the law of God in the inner man, but I see a different law in the members of my body, waging war against the law of my mind, and making me a prisoner of the law of sin which is in my members.
>
> (Romans 7:18-23)

Knowing the good is one thing. *Deciding* to do the good is another. *Actually doing* the good that is willed is still another. Some sin may result from our being closed off from the truth of God. Most sin, however, comes to those who know what is right and do not properly exercise the will to do it (James 4:17). Paul, as he dramatizes a common human situation in the seventh chapter of Romans, finds that he knows what he ought to do and, in his mind, he wills to do it, but he just does not seem to be able to carry it off. He finds himself in a civil war, his will to do the right pitted against the will to sin. He really wants to do the good. His will is not really at odds with God. But he finds himself, it seems, incapable of doing the right. It almost seems as if sin has taken over and taken him captive, despite his good desires and intentions.

Is there any way out when we find ourselves in this deadly situation? Most assuredly, but not in ourselves. God alone provides the way. "Thanks be to God through Jesus Christ our Lord!" (Romans 7:24, 25). Victory is in God alone, through Jesus Christ.

Romans 8 is a grand development of the theme that with God's help alone it is possible for us to bring our wills, our minds, our spirits, and our bodies into conformity with the will of God. Paul emphasizes that the Spirit comes to our aid and "helps our weakness" (Romans 8:26) and that He "causes all things to work together for good to those who love God, to those who are called according to His purpose" (Romans 8:28).

Not long ago, I was talking with a student who expressed a common idea. She said that she had some very sinful habits that she wanted to overcome. She wanted to conquer them before she came to God. When she was good enough, then she could come before God and accept Jesus. That is precisely what Satan would like for us to think. He wants us to think that we must overcome him on our own before we ally ourselves with God. He knows that if he can make us believe that, then we will never be able to break his hold on us. Struggling in our own power, we become disappointed with ourselves, discouraged, and hopeless. Yet, the power of God is available to us; we must allow His Spirit to enter us by accepting God's provision for our lives (Zechariah 4:6).

63

Jesus came to destroy the works of the devil (1 John 3:8). Through Jesus God has delivered us from Satan's dominion and made us citizens of the kingdom of God. "For He delivered us from the domain of darkness, and transferred us to the kingdom of His beloved Son, in whom we have redemption, the forgiveness of sins" (Colossians 1:13, 14). We *can* overcome, for God, our ally, is greater than "he who is in the world" (1 John 4:4).

Our strength is in the Lord and in the power of His might to protect us (Ephesians 6:10). By ourselves we are no match for Satan, but armed with His strength we need not  fear anything that Satan may throw at us. Paul used the metaphor of a soldier's armor to illustrate God's protective armament for those who trust in Him. He wrote, "Put on the *full* armor of God, that you may be able to stand firm against the schemes of the devil" (Ephesians 6:11). Perhaps, as Paul sat chained beside his Roman guards, he noted the defensive clothing that had been designed to protect the man from death in battle. His mind drifted to God's provision for the protection of the inner man. He urged the Ephesians to put on the *whole* armor of God. A soldier would be foolish to go into battle with only a breastplate or only a helmet or only a sword. The armor was designed as a unit to protect *all* vital areas of the soldier. As long as he was unprotected in one vital area, he was vulnerable to death. God provides a full armor and we must put on *every piece* of that armor if we are going to be victorious in the fray.

Satan is our enemy. He is a schemer. He has a strategy designed to "waste" us. He is powerful—more powerful than we, by ourselves, can ever be. "For our struggle is not against flesh and blood, but against the rulers, against the powers, against the world forces of this darkness, against the spiritual forces of wickedness in the heavenly places" (Ephesians 6:12). It is, in fact, a struggle of monumental proportions. Alone, we are over-matched. Partially armed, we will be overcome. But with the full armor of God, we will be able to stand our ground when things are at their worst (Ephesians 6:13).

The first two components of our defensive apparel are the belt of truth and the breastplate of righteousness (Ephesians 6:14). Most of us know, at least in a general way, how a Roman breastplate was put on. We've seen enough Roman movies for that. But how about this business of girding your loins? Have you girded any loins lately?

The Roman soldier wore a short skirt. Over this he wore a longer cloak that was held at the waist by a wide belt. Nobody in his right mind entered battle with the long tunic flopping around his legs to slow him down or trip him up. As a battle approached, the soldiers carefully tucked the long outer covering up so that they would be free of encumbrance. The belt that frees us from encumbrance is *truth*. The girdle that keeps us from tripping is God's truth. Jesus said to the cynical Pilate, "Everyone who is of the

truth hears My voice" (John 18:37). The words of Jesus are truth. God is truth; therefore, He is the standard by which truth is to be judged. Truth is the enemy of Satan. It exposes Satan as the liar he is. Truth encircles the believer and keeps him from falling. One of the most important preparations for our encounters with Satan is our acquisition of God's truth.

The Christian wears the breastplate of *righteousness*. Goodness, integrity, moral rectitude, and right standing with God cover his heart. Righteousness is not something of his own accomplishment. Like truth, it comes from God (Philippians 3:9). It comes by faith. Our righteousness is the gift of God through Jesus Christ (Romans 5:17).

For his sandals, the Christian wears promptness or readiness produced by the good news of *peace*. The sandals of the soldier were of utmost importance. In the days of Paul, of course, the army moved from place to place on foot. Even today, any foot soldier will tell you of the vital importance of a good pair of boots. Good sandals made it possible for the soldier to go without pain to the place where he was needed. They made it possible for him to do what was required of him after he arrived. They were a part of his equipment for readiness.

Good sandals were necessary if a soldier was to be able to stand his ground effectively. Rough terrain, hostile locale, rocky ground, these were no threat to the effectiveness of the well-shod foot soldier. Military strategists are fond of the word "mobility." That is what Paul was talking about. The Christian soldier is shod with calm courage. His morale is high because he knows that God is with him. He has a peace during adversity that non-Christians cannot understand. Paul wrote to the Philippians, "And the peace of God, which surpasses all comprehension, shall *guard* your hearts and your minds in Christ Jesus" (Philippians 4:7). God's peace will keep us from anxiety of the emotions and tensions of the mind. Our peace is Christ (Ephesians 2:14; John 14:27). Zecharias, filled with the Holy Spirit, spoke of Jesus who was given by God "to guide our feet into the way of peace" (Luke 1:79). The Greek word for peace suggests unity or concord. It comes very close to our expression about a person who "has it all together." The Christian is a bearer of the good news of togetherness, wholeness, stability, unity, completeness, reconciliation. As Isaiah put it, "How lovely on the mountains are the feet of him who brings good news, who announces peace" (Isaiah 52:7).

Satan is a disrupter, a sower of dissension, dissatisfaction, and disaster. God sends the Christian forth into the world walking the path of peace, spreading good news of reconciliation.

The first three items of our defensive equipment are spoken of as already having been put on. We are to stand firm, *having prepared* ourselves beforehand for the battle by equipping ourselves with truth, righteousness, and peace—*"having girded, having put on, having shod."* One must begin the battle against Satan well before the actual point of confrontation, the testing tree, makes its appearance. Just as a soldier begins a long time before the actual point of contact with the enemy to make preparations, the Christian completes his preparations in truth, righteousness, and peace before the moment of confrontation with the evil one. We ought also to note that there seems to be a progression. We start our preparation with God's truth, we then know how to live righteously, and then we experience God's peace.

Jesus described himself as "the way, the truth, and the life" (John 14:6). These three directly parallel the defensive armor Christ provides. The *way* corresponds with the sandals for the path of peace. The *truth* parallels our belt of truth. The *life* parallels the breastplate of good living. Jesus is our armor. We put on peace, truth, and righteousness when we put on Christ (Romans 13:14). Our preparation for battle, then, involves clothing ourselves with Jesus.

The Christian's shield is *faith.* The Greek word Paul chose for shield does not suggest a small, round shield that is swung easily around in hand-to-hand combat. It refers to the large oblong shield that a heavily-armed soldier carried. This great shield was made of two large sections of wood, and the soldier could protect himself behind it from the flaming spears thrown by the enemy. It was not designed for easy mobility so much as it was designed for maximum protection. The wood worked to extinguish the flame of the spear. The spearhead sank into the wood and thus extinguished  the spear tipped with flaming pitch. Faith, as we have noted earlier, is a prime defense against Satan's attack. It is not mere acknowledgment that Jesus existed; it is acting boldly on the basis of belief. Because of our firm commitment to Jesus, Satan cannot unsettle us with his dramatic, showy, flaming weapons. They fizzle, snuffed out by God's defensive armor in Christ. Faith, indeed, is the victory (1 John 5:4).

The helmet is *salvation.* The helmet is the head covering.

It is of vital importance, for our heads, our minds, are the targets of the enemy. The helmet of salvation helps us "keep our heads straight." Paul is not talking only about a salvation that is past. He is talking also about being saved from Satan's future attacks as well. He is talking about the "hope of salvation" (1 Thessalonians 5:8). Paul seems to be having us look forward to the day of Christ's return. It is that hope that enables us to evaluate properly the importance of events and causes today. We must judge all things in the light of the coming Lord and in light of our salvation through Him.

Finally, in his hand, the fully armed soldier of God carries the *sword of the Spirit,* the Word of God. The sword is both defensive and offensive armor. It is useful to protect us from the thrusts of the enemy and it is essential to our overcoming of him. We have noted earlier how closely faith, hope, and love, our defensive bulwarks, are linked with the Holy Spirit and the Word of God. The Holy Spirit is Christ's person and power in us. The Spirit and the Word take the initiative to defend us and to cut to pieces the lies of Satan. Jesus wielded the sword of the Word against Satan, quoting Scripture that exposed his deceptions. As we rightly wield the Word, it is able to pierce the hearts of others around us as well. The Word of God is truth in action.

For the word of God is living and active and sharper than any two-edged sword, and piercing as far as the division of soul and spirit, of both joints and marrow, and able to judge the thoughts and intentions of the heart.

(Hebrews 4:12)

The Word of God is able to reveal, even to us, the true meaning of our thoughts and intentions so that Satan cannot use our human rationalizations against us, as he did with Eve. Satan has nothing in his scabbard or quiver to match the Word of God.

The Christian must give much attention to being practiced in the Word. Swordmanship must constantly be worked at. We must "work out" with the Word, making the weapon our own. **No matter how lethal a weapon is, if we are not familiar with it, it has little strategic value for us.**

The sword suggests two-way communication. Paul relates it to God's direction of man through His Word. But with his mention of the Spirit, Paul turns his mind to prayer, man's communication with God. That spiritual union with God is to be continuing and conscious. The same Spirit who inspired the Word indwells the Christian to help him (Romans 8:9). The Christian is to be alert, watchful, patient, and persevering. His prayers and petitions are not to be only for himself. They are also to be for others. An important part of his prayer for others, in the Spirit, should be that they might have *boldness* in the gospel. Prayer, then, is an offensive weapon of great power as it unites us with God and with His people for the battle. The Christian must be constant, intense, and unselfish in his prayers. There is great strength in a praying community of saints. The sword of the Spirit, the true Word of God, and watchful prayer equip the Christian to take the battle to the enemy. Both are combined in the Spirit and are intended for boldness in the day of battle. The Word is of no value if it is merely known. It must be exercised and applied to the individual life. Likewise prayer must be applied to the individual need.

Faith, hope of salvation, the Word of God, and prayer all

69

are the continuing characteristics of the Christian who dwells within God's maximum security. Like the other pieces of armor, they all find their meaning in Christ.

The book of 1 John contains some of the most triumphant passages in the New Testament. The triumphant triad rings throughout the passages, particularly chapters 4 and 5, like joyous bells in a glorious peal of praises to God. Space permits us to note only a few of the glorious melody lines.

> Beloved, let us *love* one another, for *love* is from God; and everyone who *loves* is *born of God* and knows God. The one who does not *love* does not know God, for God is *love.* By this the *love* of God was manifested in us, that God has sent His only begotten Son into the world *so that we might live through Him* [hope].... if we *love* one another, *God abides in us,* and His *love* is perfected in us. By this we know that we abide in Him and He in us, because *He has given us of His Spirit.* . . . Whoever confesses that Jesus is the Son of God, *God abides in him, and he in God* [faith] and we have *come to know* and *have believed* [faith] the *love* which God has for us. God is *love,* and the one who abides in *love* abides in God, and *God abides in him* [love]. By this, *love* is perfected with us, that *we may have confidence in the day of judgment* [hope]; because as He is, so also are we in this world. [We are allied, and thus possess His strength.] There is no fear in *love* [not even Satan can harm us]; but perfect *love* casts out fear [hope], because fear involves punishment, and the one who fears is not perfected in *love* [hope]. . . . And this commandment we have from Him, that the one who *loves* God should *love* his brother also. *Whoever believes that Jesus is the Christ is born of God* [has God's nature in him]; and whoever *loves* the Father *loves* the child born of Him. By this we know that we *love* the children of God, when we *love* God and *observe His commandments.* For this is the *love* of God, that we *keep His commandments; and His commandments are not burdensome.* For whatever is *born of God* [see John 3:1-21] *overcomes the world* [hope]; and this is the *victory* that has overcome the world—our *faith.* And who is the one who overcomes the world, but he who believes that Jesus is the Son of God?
>
> (1 John 4:7—5:5)

Then we come to a passage that the commentator Plummer describes as one of the most perplexing passages in the New Testament. We are told that Jesus "came by water and blood" and that these, along with the Spirit, in agreement, bear witness concerning God's Son, that God has given us eternal life in Him. Water we immediately

70

associate with Jesus' birth, His baptism, and His crucifixion. Baptism portrays a birth and a death (Romans 6:1-14). Jesus' earthly ministry began with His baptism when the Spirit descended like a dove upon Him and the voice of God said, "This is My beloved Son, in whom I am well-pleased" (Matthew 3:17). It ended with the water and blood gushing from His side on the cross (John 19:34).

The blood would seem to refer to the cross where Jesus, firmly within the will of God, died for the sins of mankind. The Spirit evidently speaks of God's presence with Jesus throughout His lifetime and His promised presence in the lives of those who become His people. Is it possible that in this difficult passage we once again find our triumphant triad—faith, hope, and love? Certainly the witness of the blood would speak of God's love in Christ, who suffered the death of the cross that we might have everlasting life (John 3:16). The water, perhaps, speaks of faith (Mark 16:16). Jesus began His ministry with unswerving acceptance of the will of God. Something special happens at baptism. In the early church, baptism was the response of adults. Those who come to receive it come to make a complete break with the past and confess their faith by being buried in the water to die with Christ (Romans 6:1-14). In Christ, one is reborn into a new life and becomes a new creature. At baptism, God's love in Christ and man's faith in the Lord Jesus meet, and a wonderful alliance takes place. The Spirit comes to dwell in the life of the individual in such a way that it is possible to speak of the body as the temple of God (1 Corinthians 6:19, 20). The Spirit would seem to correspond with hope, for it is God's seal for the present and future (2 Corinthians 1:22; Ephesians 1:13).

Here, then, we seem to see the *blood* of Jesus (love) blocking Satan's advance through the lust of the flesh. We see the unseen reality of faith enacted in baptism. The new person emerges from baptism with new values and priorities because Christ is now in him—blocking Satan in the area of the lust of the eyes. And finally we see the Spirit, sent by God to work with the believer in alliance (hope) against Satan's wiles so that he is able to be victorious on all fronts connected with the pride of life.

The blood, the water, and the Spirit all bear witness of

Jesus, testifying that He has provided for our new birth and new life. They are in agreement. They interlock for our defense and salvation (1 John 5:8). God has clearly borne witness of Jesus through the blood, water, and Spirit. If we believe in Jesus, the power of these witnesses comes within us (1 John 5:10). God's witness to us and His witness in us through faith unite to trumpet a glorious message of hope, "God has given us eternal life, and this life is in His Son" (1 John 5:11).

John continues,

> "These things I have written to you who *believe* in the name of the Son of God, in order that you may know that you have eternal life [*hope*]. And this is the confidence [*faith*] which we have before Him, that, if we ask anything according to His will, He hears us [*faith, hope*]. And if we know that He hears us in whatever we ask, we know that we have the requests which we have asked from Him [*faith, hope*]. . . . We know that no one who is born of God [*loves God (1 John 4:7) and believes (5:1, 4)*] sins; but He who was born of God [*Jesus*] keeps him [*through His Holy Spirit*] and the evil one does not touch him [*victory*]."
>
> (1 John 5:13-15, 18)

The verses of 1 John 5:16-18 are difficult, open to a number of interpretations. We have there the contrast of those who are abiding in the faith, hope, and love of God and those who deliberately reject God's defenses. If we are abiding in the citadel of Christ, protected by His strength, encompassed by His Spirit, allied in faith, hope, and love with Him, it is possible that we may lose some battles with Satan without losing the war. It is possible that we will, in our conceit and self-interest, sally forth from God's protection and be defeated by Satan. It is possible that we will sin. If we return to our faithful Ally with repentance, prayer, and love of God, we have His *forgiving strength* to put Satan to flight. But if we deliberately forsake His citadel, if we deliberately abandon His protective shield of the Spirit, if we encamp with Satan and become his ally out of choice, if we desert to the other side and, with full acceptance of Satan, take our place with his forces, then we have placed ourselves beyond the wall of God.

To join Satan's forces is to join the army of death. Death is already in us, rather than the eternal life that is in us when we are in God and His Spirit. We have utterly capitulated. And even more, we have joined in battle with God on Satan's side. The "sin not leading to death" (1 John 5:16, 17) is probably the occasional sortie into sin by the person who intends to be obedient to God. When he falls, he humbly admits his failures to God so that God can forgive him. He is momentarily overcome by his desires, his laziness, or his rebellious spirit. He sincerely wants to remain within the perimeter of God's battleline, but he momentarily is caught outside the lines and is defeated. He is a sin-straggler who flees back to God's lines determined not to be caught outside the camp of God again.

If we see one of our human allies, one of our brothers, caught outside God's camp, John would have us pray earnestly for him that he might be snatched from the evil one and returned to the army of life. "If anyone sees his brother committing a sin not leading to death, he shall ask and God will for him give life to those who commit sin not leading to death" (1 John 5:16). John makes it clear that prayer is an essential ingredient to our comradeship-in-arms against the evil one. It is the Christian's method of fighting back, of rescuing the straggler, of maintaining contact with the will of the Commander.

If, however, our brother becomes a deserter, if he begins to boast of his sin without shame, if he delights in his rebellion against God and boasts of his ability to get away with it, if he willingly accepts the command of Satan and makes sin his standard, then he is no longer an endangered ally in need of prayerful help, but an enemy for whom not even prayer can any longer avail.

Let us describe this process, visualizing God's kingdom as a castle. While within its walls, we are safe and secure. One day, however, we venture out the gate of the lust of the flesh and enter into sin. We rush back, guilty and sorrowful, throwing ourselves on the love of God, which prevents Satan from taking us captive. Later, however, we decide that that was pretty adventurous of us, taking on Satan by ourselves. We remember that we came out of it pretty well, even if a bit humbled. And our prideful spirit focuses on the humiliation of having to admit to God that we had strayed outside His lines. We wonder if perhaps there are some really good things outside the castle that we are missing. We look down and Satan's forces seem to be having such a good time. We sally forth again, saying that we are going to do battle. But we join the revel. Satan tells us that we are obviously no longer welcome back in the castle. He says the gates are closed. And besides, we've only begun to sample Satan's fun. Soon we find ourselves locked into the dance of death. The castle is closed to us, not because of God's will, but because we are now, as disciples of the devil, no longer willing to try the gates ourselves.

Hebrews 6:4-6 is important to us in understanding this principle.

> For in the case of those who have once been enlightened and have tasted the heavenly gift and have been made partakers of the Holy Spirit, and have tasted the good *word of God* and the powers of the age to come, and then have fallen away [*deserted and joined the enemy*], it is impossible to renew them to repentance [*They, blinded by Satan, view the open gates as closed gates so that they make no effort to return to the citadel of God.*], since they again crucify to themselves the Son of God [*They are at war with God.*], and put Him to open shame [*They reject His power to save.*]."
>
> (Hebrews 6:4-6)

Joining the enemy after we have become Christians breaks God's heart. It shames the cross by robbing it of its redemptive power in our lives, it mocks the church by bringing discredit upon its role in the life of the believer.

If we fulfill the will of God who made us, we receive rich blessings from God. We dwell within His protection. His arms overshadow us (Psalm 91). But if we willfully choose not to return to the One who provides for our defense and growth, we will receive the reward of our disobedience (Hebrews 6:7, 8). The writer to the Hebrews says somewhat later,

> And we desire that each one of you show the same diligence so as to realize the full assurance of *hope* until the end, that you may not be sluggish, but imitators of those who through *faith* and patience [*enduring love*] inherit the promises [*hope*].
>
> (Hebrews 6:11, 12)

First John closes with the battle cry of the faithful, who

are safe and secure in God and beyond the reach of the power of the evil one.

> We know that we are of God, and the whole world lies in the power of the evil one. And we know [*faith*] that the Son of God has come, and has given us understanding [*faith*], in order that we might know Him who is true [*faith*], and we are in Him who is true, in His Son Jesus Christ [*love, faith, hope*]. This is the true God and eternal life [*hope*].
>
> (1 John 5:19, 20)

Chapter Six

YOU & ME
At the Testing Tree
(2 Corinthians 4, 5, 6; 1 Corinthians 10; James 1;
1 Peter 5; Hebrews 12)

Here I am at my testing trees. They loom before me, arching over me with their intertwined branches, blocking out the sun and obscuring my vision. The tree of failure. The tree of pain. The tree of grief. The tree of loss. The tree of alienation. The tree of disappointment. The tree of misunderstanding. The tree of illness. The tree of rejection. The tree of remorse. The tree of misfortune. The tree of tragedy. The tree of indecision. The tree of insecurity. The tree of frustration. The tree of trouble. The tree of sorrow. The tree of neediness. The tree of aging. The tree of death.

Sometimes I wish that God would bulldoze them all from my life so that I could be rid of them once and for all. I wonder why He permits *me* to suffer. Oh, I can explain it for others. I can talk about how suffering, trials, and tribulation can work good in peoples' lives. I see examples of that all around me. But I find it pretty hard to look on the bright side when *my* sun is blocked out by the fretful foliage of ill fortune. Satan, as is his wont, has me looking the wrong way. He is able to block out my sun because I have blocked out the Son.

Paul realized that unbelief gives Satan opportunity to keep the light of the glorious gospel of Christ from shining on us. He wrote, "The spirit of this world has blinded the minds of those who do not believe, and prevents the light of the glorious gospel of Christ, the image of God, from shining on them" (2 Corinthians 4:4, Phillips*). The believer, however, is not destined to grope in the murky depths of a dark forest of despair. God, the author of light, has sent a light to penetrate the darkest depths of anguish in ourselves and others. "For God, who said, 'Light shall shine out of darkness,' is the One who has shone in our hearts to give the light of the knowledge of the glory of God in the face of Christ" (2 Corinthians 4:6). It is this glorious light of the good news of Christ that fills us with God's power to overcome whatever distress life brings. It is mindboggling to think that through faith in Christ, through acceptance of the "glorious gospel of Christ," through knowledge of the glory of God seen in Jesus, we possess within us, in these fragile, mortal, humble bodies of ours, *the very power of God!* Paul wrote, "We have this treasure in earthen vessels, that the surpassing greatness of the power may be of God and not from ourselves" (2 Corinthians 4:7).

When he encountered dejection and defeat in himself and others, Paul remembered that the believer possesses a high office. He is an ambassador of Christ (2 Corinthians 5:20), God's highly honored and divinely safeguarded representative, to carry the good news of reconciliation (return to freedom within the boundaries of God's will) to God. Paul was keenly aware that whatever goodness he possessed was not of his own creation. Rather it was the accomplishment of Christ, who took Paul's sin upon himself. Christ, Paul knew, is in all things an Ally (2 Corinthians 6:1), who both listens and helps.

Paul learned how to accept good things—and bad—with joy. He experienced more than his share of testing trees: afflictions, hardships, distresses, beatings, imprisonments, tumults, labors, sleeplessness, hunger, dishonor, evil report, falsehood about himself, sorrow, poverty, and destitution.

---

*Phillips—The New Testament in Modern English, ©1958, J.B. Phillips (New York: Macmillan Company, 1960).

Yet, with Christ's help, from these he learned purity, knowledge, patience, kindness, and love (2 Corinthians 6:4-10).

Though my outer man finds it hard to accept the benefit of testing, my inner man *does* profit from trials, as long as I meet them with the strength and protection of God's power in me. The Bible abounds with teaching on the benefits of suffering, trials, and tribulation. They are disciplining, beneficial gifts of our loving Heavenly Father (Hebrews 12:6-11).

If this is true, ought I therefore to seek opportunities for the strengthening that trials bring by asking God for more trials in my life? If temptation is testing that can be an occasion for victory, should I then pray, *"Lead me into temptation"*? In that way I could strengthen my inner man by repeated conflict with and victory over Satan. I could demonstrate my faith, hope, and love in actual practice despite difficult circumstances. And if this is so, why did Jesus give precisely the opposite model for His disciples when He taught them about prayer? He urged them to pray, "And do not lead us into temptation, but deliver us from evil" (Matthew 6:13).

If temptation/testing is in actual fact an opportunity for blessing, why the negative in the model prayer? Ought we not rather to pray more along the lines of the prayer of the Psalmist?

> Search me, O God, and know my heart;
> Try me [this is the Hebrew word for *test* or *tempt*]
>   and know my anxious thoughts;
> And see if there be any hurtful way in me,
> And lead me in the everlasting way.
>
> (Psalm 139:23, 24)

For all their obvious possibility for benefit, testings and trials are not pleasant experiences for anyone. They accomplish great good, but they are a painful school for sanctity. Jesus, who experienced intense testing, knows our feelings very well in this regard. He knows that the loving chastening of the Lord is designed for our benefit, but He also knows that it can be a painful experience for us human beings to undergo.

79

Jesus knew pain. He knew testing. As He approached the supreme testing tree of His life, the cross, He himself prayed, "My Father, if it is possible, let this cup pass from Me; yet not as I will, but as Thou wilt" (Matthew 26:39). On that night, He spoke lovingly to His disciples, saying, "Keep watching and praying that you may not enter into temptation . . ." (Matthew 26:41). The spirit, He noted, was willing to do this, but the flesh was weak. The inner man wanted to be alert and watchful in prayer for the intense, personal trials that lay ahead, but the body, which is so important to carrying out the purposes of the inner man and which often suffers greatly in trials, was weak.

If the model prayer is similar to Jesus' prayer in Gethsemane, then it may be saying, "Please, God, don't lead me into testing if there is any other way for me to be what You want me to be. But I'm content to accept and thank You for what You want in my life."

Then too, when I ask God, as in the model prayer, not to lead me into temptation/testing, I am asking Him to make me such a person that testing will not be necessary for me. I am asking Him to develop in me such inner strength, such reliance on Him, such firm commitment to His will, and such confident dependence on His provision for my life that God's chastening will no longer be necessary for me. I will *already possess* the self-control and patient reliance on God that trouble and tribulation are designed to teach. Seen in this light, the model prayer is saying, "Lead me in such a way that my love, faith, and hope are so strong that I will no longer need temptation to develop them."

In any case, I do not need to seek occasion to demonstrate my faithfulness in tribulation. There will be enough opportunity for that without my intentionally seeking it. It is within the realm of our sovereign God to decide when and for what reasons He will allow tests to be apportioned to us. We dare not flirt with trouble.

It is interesting to note that while the first part of the petition of the model prayer asks God not to lead us into testing, the second part of it addresses itself to our situation once we find ourselves in testing. There we are to request God to "deliver us from evil" or to "deliver us from the evil one." Finding ourselves in trial and testing, we are to ask

God to work in us and with us to overcome Satan's power and turn our testing trees into trees of triumph.

The two clauses of the model prayer, when taken together, seek God's sustaining help. "If possible," we pray, "help us to be such that trials will not be necessary to perfect us. But be on our side in the trials that do come so that we together with You may defeat the evil one." We are not seeking so much to be delivered *from* temptation as to be delivered *during* it.

God is watchful in my trials. He is faithful. Sometimes I feel that my trials are too heavy to bear, that no one has been called upon to experience what I have had to experience. But God's Word tells me that "No temptation has overtaken you but such as is common to man" (1 Corinthians 10:13). What seems unique and beyond bearing to me is in the common run of things. I frequently get my mind so firmly set on my troubles that I cannot put them into a wider perspective. But God reminds me to do just that. Further, God's Word promises, "God is faithful, who will not allow you to be tempted beyond what you are able" (1 Corinthians 10:13). God wants my temptations and my trials to cleanse me, not to crush me. He wants them to strengthen me, not to suffocate me. So He does not allow them to be overpowering. He created me. He knows my characteristics and my limitations.

Let us imagine a glass factory where high-grade crystal is blown. In the factory are a number of workers whose job it is to oversee the quality of the finished crystal. There are a number of ways they can do that, but it is doubtful that they will set a crystal goblet on a table and smash it with a sledgehammer to see how clear it is.

I WONDER IF THIS CRYSTAL GOBLET IS ANY GOOD?

The test would not be appropriate to the nature of the tested object. No matter how pure the crystal was, it could not withstand such a test. In a similar way, God does not test us with inappropriate tests, tests completely beyond our capacities for coping. Any temptation that comes my way carries a guarantee that I can handle it *with God's help.*

In the same package with temptation/testing is God's provision for handling it. With the temptation, God "will provide a way of escape also, that you may be able to endure it" (1 Corinthians 10:13). The Bible does not say here that the "way of escape" is necessarily the immediate cessation of the test. Rather, God gives us the ability to endure, to hang on, to pass through to victory. I think that the "way of escape" is our triumphant triad: faith, hope, and love. These are both our defense and our sustaining strength in the face of trials.

The passage we have been considering nestles within some others that call to mind Israel's disobedience in the wilderness, as the children of Israel tried God (1 Corinthians 10:9). Paul, urging the believers to watchfulness, wrote, "Therefore let him who thinks he stands take heed lest he fall" (1 Corinthians 10:12). Prideful smugness is ever the tool of the evil one.

Having educated the Corinthians on God's loving protection from testing overkill and His provision for deliverance through endurance, Paul gives valuable instruction in the rest of chapter 10:   1. Flee idolatry (1 Corinthians 10:14). Make the only true God the center of your whole allegiance. 2. Shun the spiritual forces that oppose God (10:20, 21). 3. Seek the good of others (10:24, 33). 4. Make all your actions glorify God (10:31). 5. Imitate Christ (11:1). 6. Hold on to the divine revelation of God (11:2).

But what happens at the testing tree when I capitulate to Satan? What happens if I allow him to lead me down the wooded path of sin? What can I do to find my way back to the protection of God? What do I do when I stand soul-sick with the bitter awareness of guilt churning in my stomach and God's voice within me saying, "What is this you have done?" (Genesis 3:13). How do I handle my sin and guilt? Some people try to handle guilt by eliminating God from their consciousness. They try to discredit the Scriptures and silence the voice of God whispering of right and wrong within them. They make man the standard of all things and remove any absolute standard by which they must judge their thoughts and actions. Or, knowing that something in their lives is seriously wrong, they try to find someone outside themselves to blame. "To err is human . . ." so the saying goes. And to blame it on someone else is even more human! Eve blamed her disobedience on Satan and on God, who made the serpent. Adam blamed the woman and God, who made her. We follow in their wake (and wakes are associated with funerals as well as with boats).

"To err is human,
To blame it on
someone else is
even more human".

There are three major possibilities for blame. I can blame God, I can blame Satan (claiming that I am not responsible because he overpowered me with his superior abilities), or I can shoulder the responsibility myself. James spoke about the first course when he wrote, "Let no one say when he is tempted, 'I am being tempted by God'; for God cannot be tempted by evil, and He Himself does not tempt any one" (James 1:13). This statement seems to run somewhat counter to Scriptures that indicate that God *does* test His human creation. Abraham, as we have noted earlier, was tested by God (Genesis 22:1). God chastens us as a father does his beloved children (Hebrews 12:5-11). God has designed testing, as we have frequently noted, for our benefit.

In the New American Standard Bible, the words translated "trial" and "tempted" in James 1:12-14 are from the same Greek root. James, I think, was not saying that God does not ever try us, so much as he was saying that we cannot use the fact that He does as an excuse to evade responsibility for our actions when we fail at the point of testing. James wrote, "*Let no one say* when he is tempted, 'I am being tempted by God' " (James 1:13). He was saying, in effect, "*Let no one say* when he is being tested, 'I am the helpless pawn of God in this. I am the victim. My actions are beyond my ken and control. Everything was destined by God, who created me to do what I do, even to do the sin that I do.' " To say this is wrong for two reasons, "for God cannot be tempted by evil, and He Himself does not tempt any one." God and evil are incompatible. Therefore, He cannot be the source of evil. Evil is alien to His nature. He cannot be enticed by it. It holds no allure for Him. It offers no test for His nature. It never gets inside Him; so it never can come out of Him. And "He Himself does not tempt anyone." God does not test anyone with the intent that he sin. He tests him with the intent that he conquer. I cannot blame God for the evil in my life. God designed nothing with the intent that it produce evil. Rather, the tests of life are designed by God to produce good. He does not test anyone by evil, for evil, being incompatible with His nature, does not spring from Him. He does, however, test and try His human creation with tests appropriate to the nature of man and his needs. Evil is not an artifact of the will and knowledge of God. Its prime source is elsewhere.

If not God, then perhaps Satan, the deceiver, the evil one, overpowered me. Perhaps Satan made me sin. He is a celestial being of great cunning and power. But the passage we considered earlier, 1 Corinthians 10:13, closes that excuse to me. I cannot claim innocence because I was swept away by a power beyond my ability to resist. God will not permit that, unless I choose to reject His saving provision. Satan has the ability to conquer only if I give it to him by rejecting God's assistance. God provides a test with the way out, if I will simply rely on Him for it. Satan does not make us do evil, but he is skillful at giving us reasons for doing what we want to do—disobey God.

No, it is not God who is responsible for my sin. Nor am I carried away beyond my powers of escape by Satan. I must, finally, admit that I am the one who is responsible when I sin. It is my lust to which Satan makes his pitch. It is my godless desire that carries me away, that entices me into sin. My evil desires give birth to sin. And sin, when it is fully grown, produces death (James 1:14, 15). I must not let Satan deceive me in this matter. He would like nothing better than to have me blame God. Failing this, he will take responsibility himself. Proud of his power and desirous that I be intimidated and misled by it, he encourages me to play the role of the helpless victim. He knows that as long as

I play that role, I will do nothing to restore my broken relationship with God. The recognition of responsibility is the beginning of repentance, return, and reconciliation (Luke 15:18; 18:13).

Responsibility is truly mine. I cannot blame someone or something else, my environment, my heredity, my parents, or circumstances beyond my control. I must recognize that my desires are decisive. "But each one is tempted when he is carried away and enticed by his own lust. Then when lust has conceived, it gives birth to sin; and when sin is accomplished, it brings forth death" (James 1:14, 15).

God is not the author of evil. Rather, He is the author of *good gifts* (James 1:17). I am intended to be His offspring, His firstborn, His heir. It is His Word that has conceived me, that has given me life (James 1:18). It is His will that I be heir of His promises. Therefore, I am to put aside filthiness and the remains of wickedness and let God's Word combine with my humble acceptance of it (departing thus from the boastful pride of life) to produce the offspring of salvation (James 1:21).

It was God's will that I be born as His heir, conceived by the word of truth and born a new creature in Christ. This is in stark contrast to lust, which, conceived and nurtured in me, give birth to sin and death. As a new creature in Christ, I grow to maturity, putting God's Word into action. As an active doer, I am blessed richly in my life of obedience. My life-style becomes a love-style. I am concerned about the needs of others, and I work with God in erecting barriers to the intrusion of the death-style of "the world" into my life and into the lives of others (James 1:18-27).

My humility must express itself in conformity with the will of God as revealed in His Word if my salvation is to be received. Pride and arrogance are bitter foes of repentance. I do not readily want to admit that I desperately need God and what He offers me.

We frequently hear people say, "Religion is all right for those who need it." The implication is that some people can get things together without God, that He is a crutch for the weak and the infirm of the world. One who would make such a claim is confident that he is not such a person. The statement drips with pride. As long as a person persists in

85

this attitude, it is unlikely that he will experience God's riches for him. Humility is the heart-soil in which the Word of God can take root (Philippians 2:5-11). Or, to change the metaphor, it is the seed that can be fertilized by the Word of God. Humility before God makes it possible for us to become doers of the will of God as revealed in the Word of God. If we congratulate ourselves that we are not as other men, there is little hope of our returning to the will of God. Our attitude must be, "God, be merciful to me, *the sinner!*" (Luke 18:13, 14). Strangely enough, true freedom is possible for us only as we walk within the limitations of God (James 1:25).

Peter warned, "God is opposed to the proud, but gives grace to the humble. Humble yourselves, therefore, under the mighty hand of God, that He may exalt you at the proper time, casting all your anxiety upon Him, because He cares for you" (1 Peter 5:5-7). We endure trial, knowing that God cares for us. Since He carries our worry and anxiety, we do not need to carry them ourselves.

If we are going to turn testing into triumph, we must make a firm stand against Satan. "Be self-controlled and vigilant always, for your enemy the devil is always about, prowling like a lion roaring for its prey. Resist him, standing firm in your *faith,* remembering that the strain is the same for all your fellow-Christians in other parts of the world. And after you have borne these sufferings a very little while, the God of all grace, who has called you to share his eternal splendour through Christ, will himself make you whole and secure and strong" (1 Peter 5:8-10, Phillips).

Satan is no match for the one who trusts in God and who resists Satan with the power of Christ within him. Satan makes a big show, roaring about. He is hungry for us, but his roar is all bluff. A really dangerous lion stalks its quarry *quietly.* Satan, the great deceiver, pretends he is powerful and advertises his greatness, seeking to frighten us into submission by his deceitful roar. Yet, we have power to send him running with his tail between his legs, as we resist, energized by firm faith in Jesus. We will suffer for a time, perhaps, but it is short in comparison to the eternal glory that God promises in Christ to those who overcome. God uses these testings to complete us, to make us secure in

Christ, and to make us strong in the inner person (1 Peter 5:10). God's dominion is forever. His power, authority, and rule are absolute. Satan, the imposter, pretends that he is "king of the jungle" but he is actually "coward of the forest" before the strength of God in us. We need not fear him in the least (1 Peter 5:11).

There is a great deal more that could be said about temptation. We have seen that testing, trials, tribulation, and temptation can work for good in our lives if we use them as occasions for relying on the will of God. Satan comes into the moment of testing, attempting to turn testing into rebellion against the will of God. He seeks to accomplish this by capitalizing on three areas of our nature, the lust of the flesh, the lust of the eyes, and the boastful pride of life. We can resist him on these fronts with the defenses of God: love to counter the lust of the flesh, faith to counter the lust of the eyes, and hope to counter the pride of life. These three bulwarks are both God's gifts to us and our responses to Him. They offer secure defense. God's Spirit and His Word reinforce us and direct us in our defense. God's grace provides all that we need to overcome the evil one.

If we are having trouble resisting Satan, we cannot overcome by constructing a temporary defense against him. We cannot conquer him by making New Year's resolutions or giving ourselves lectures on self-control. What is required is absolute trust in the goodness of God and in His wisdom for our lives. What is needed is a complete recognition of the sovereignty of God for our lives. Rather than conforming to the pattern of the present world, we must adapt ourselves to God, letting Him remake our minds and transform our whole natures until we are able to discern that His will for us is good, acceptable, and perfect. We must first humble ourselves, assessing our importance not by worldly standards but by the worth that God has given us through the faith He has made possible for us. Then we must exercise God's gifts, freely given to us by the grace of God. We must have genuine love. We must seek righteousness. There must be a real break with evil and a real devotion to good. Humble, diligent, zealous, energetic, prayerful, generous, forgiving, sympathetic, harmonious, unassuming, honorable, noble, peaceable, the Christian does not permit evil to overpower him. Rather, he takes the initiative, overpowering evil with good (Romans 12; read the Phillips translation).

In all that I am doing, I must remember that I live at a critical moment. I must be aware and watchful. Every day brings God's salvation nearer, and I must be ready for Christ's return.

> The night is almost gone, and the day is at hand. Let us behave properly as in the day, not in carousing and drunkenness, not in sexual promiscuity and sensuality, not in strife and jealousy. But put on the Lord Jesus Christ, and make no provision for the flesh in regard to its lusts.
>
> (Romans 13:12-14)

Paul wrote to the Thessalonians,

> But we should always give thanks to God for you, brethren beloved by the Lord, because God has chosen you from the beginning for salvation through sanctification by the Spirit and faith in the truth. And it was for this He called you through our gospel, that you may gain the glory of our Lord Jesus Christ. So then, brethren, stand firm and hold to the traditions which you were taught, whether by word of mouth or by letter from us.
>
> Now may our Lord Jesus Christ Himself and God our Father, who has loved us and given us eternal comfort and good hope by grace, comfort and strengthen your hearts in every good work and word.
>
> Finally, brethren, pray for us that the word of the Lord may spread rapidly and be glorified, just as it did also with you; and that we may be delivered from perverse and evil men; for not all have faith. But the Lord is faithful, and He will strengthen and protect you from the evil one.
>
> (2 Thessalonians 2:13—3:3)

How can we deal with the tests that come our way? Hebrews 11 is a grand gallery of heroes. These people of faith offer us models of victorious faith and trust in God. In the chapter following, Hebrews 12, the writer gives further teaching that is extremely helpful to us as we encounter the testing trees of our lives. Let's look at some of the lessons we can learn.

Be Conscious of the Greats of the Past
(Hebrews 11; 12:1)

Learn from the Scriptures the principles of victory as evidenced by the champions of the past. Realize that these very champions are cheering you on to victory (12:1). They encourage you by their example, for they overcame trials more difficult than any you are called upon to meet. They participate with you in your struggle, and their lives bear witness of the power of God to do everything He promised.

Rid Yourselves of All Encumbrances and Run Wisely
(Hebrews 12:1)

Lay aside the "weights" that hinder you. Some of these things are deliberate sins. Others are things that are not necessarily wrong, but they hinder your best effort. You are not only to run light, you are to run smart. You are to run patiently and methodically, concentrating on steady endurance so that you can reach the finish line with victory.

The champion long-distance runner may very well follow a pacesetter throughout much of the race. If you are going to live victoriously, you must follow the example and leadership of Jesus. He is both the beginning and the end of faith. If you have difficulty in your life, you need not despair. He himself endured the cross and shook off shame in order to attain the victorious position He now occupies in Heaven, where, as champion of all, He sits at the right hand of God.

"Champion" is an apt word for Jesus, for He was victorious in His earthly life and He now takes our part, or champions our cause, with God. As a runner studies a champion to improve his own form, you are to look to Jesus for an example of endurance and patient suffering. When you get weary and think you can take no more of what life seems to give you, you need to look to Him who suffered beyond what anyone else will ever suffer (Philippians 2:8-11).

Put Your Difficulties in Perspective
(Hebrews 12:4)

In light of what our predecessors have endured and what Jesus experienced, your own sufferings are slight indeed. You have problems, but you probably have not yet shed your blood for your faith. Most of your trials do not come because you are striving against sin; they too frequently come as a result of your allowing sin to take root in your life.

Remember the Fatherhood of God
(Hebrews 12:5-11)

God is not going to make your life immune from trials (Proverbs 3:11, 12). As a matter of fact, as a father trains his son with discipline and thoughtful, loving correction, so God uses the difficulties of life to build you into a strong, resilient human being. Your troubles ought to be seen as a means of Christian growth toward holiness and righteousness. The question that should come to your mind is not so much, "What have I done to deserve this?" as it should be "What lesson of eternal importance can I learn from this situation?"

Have Courage! Encourage Others
(Hebrews 12:12, 13)

It is a curious fact that in helping others, we help ourselves. Hebrews 12:13 may mean, "Run a wise course yourself; stay on the track and you will not have to worry about your legs giving out." It may also mean, "Help others. Encourage those who are weak so that they can become strong." If you take your mind off yourself and focus your energies on helping others, you find, to your amazement, that your own difficulties diminish considerably.

Run the Race of Peace and Holiness
(Hebrews 12:14)

Many of your difficulties arise because you are not willing to be a peacemaker. You frequently ask yourself, "What can I do to get my way in this situation?" when you ought to ask, "What can I do to bring peace in this situation?"

In the face of difficulty, our aim must be to look good in the eyes of God. As holy men and women, we are different from others. We are separated. The track of holiness leads into the presence of almighty God.

Keep Up with the Grace of God
(Hebrews 12:18)

Don't straggle behind. Don't drop out or dally. Let the grace of God, like a following wind, sweep you on toward victory.

Don't Get Tripped Up by the Roots of Worldliness
(Hebrews 12:15)

Don't get involved with people and things that will lead to your downfall. Much of the bitterness of life comes from our living by the world's noxious standards and not living by God's righteous leading.

Watch Out for the Sensual
(Hebrews 12:16)

Some people see nothing beyond this world and its pleasures. Like the classic example, Esau, they would give up the most important thing in order to satisfy the immediate appetite of the body. Esau threw away his inheritance for a pot of stew. You ought not to throw away the victory of eternal life to satisfy base and corrupt desires.

In the face of discouragement, despair, suffering, turmoil, and trouble, we find strength by remembering the faith and victory of those who have endured far more than we have been called upon to bear. We look to our own lives and try to rid ourselves of the encumbrances and sins that drag us down. We look to Jesus who himself was victorious. We note that, relatively speaking, our trials are yet smaller than they might be. We look within the difficulties for the teaching of God and realize that spiritual strength comes from testing and exposure to trials. We take courage, focus our attention on helping others, seek after holiness and the grace of God, and separate ourselves from the sensual appetites that would debilitate and defeat us.

TEXTS FOR TESTS

Old Testament

Genesis
2:16, 17
3:1-24
4:1-15
22:1-19

Exodus
16:4-12
17:1-7
20:20

Numbers
14:1-25
21:4-7

Deuteronomy
6:10-19
7:17-19
8:1-20
29:1-19

Judges
2:21-23

Psalms
11:4-7
19:7-14
25:12-22
34:2-22
77:1-20
78:17-72
94:1-23
95:1-11
106:13-15

Proverbs
3:1-12
9:10
17:3

Isaiah
7:12

Lamentations
3:39-42

Malachi
3:16—4:6

New Testament

Matthew
  4:1-11
  6:13
  13:36-43
  26:36-46
  28:18

Mark
  1:12, 13
  8:31-38
  14:32-42

Luke
  4:1-13
  8:4-15
  11:14-22
  22:28-32

John
  7:17
  8:34-36, 44
  12:25-31
  14:13-27, 30
  16:33
  17:13-17

Acts
  5:1-11
  26:14-18

Romans
  5:1-21
  6:11-23
  8:1-39
  12:9-21
  13:11-14
  15:4, 13, 14
  16:17-20

1 Corinthians
  1:18
  7:5
  10:6-13

2 Corinthians
  2:10, 11
  4:1-18
  5:17-21
  6:1-10
  7:1, 10
  10:3-7
  11:3, 14
  12:7-10

Galatians
  5:13-26
  6:1, 2

Ephesians
  1:18-23
  2:1-9
  3:8-21
  4:17-32
  5:1-21
  6:10-20

Philippians
  1:9,11, 18-21
  2:1-18
  3:18-21

Colossians
  1:9-29
  2:1-15
  3:12-17

1 Thessalonians
  3:4-13
  4:1-18
  5:8-22

2 Thessalonians
   1:3-12
   2:3-17

1 Timothy
   1:12-17
   6:3-21

2 Timothy
   1:7-14
   2:1-26
   4:17, 18

Titus
   2:6-15
   3:1-11

Hebrews
   2:7-18
   3:7-19
   4:12-16
   5:7-10
   6:4-6, 9-20
   8:12
   9:13, 14
   10:8-39
   11:1-40
   12:1-17

James
   1:2-25
   4:1-17

1 Peter
   1:3-25
   2:1-25
   4:1-19
   5:5-12

2 Peter
   2:1-21

1 John
   2:1-29
   3:1-24
   4:1-21
   5:1-21

2 John
   7-9

Jude
   6

Revelation
   3:9-11

STUDY BOOKS
by Ward Patterson

Triumph Over Temptation (39976). A look at the positive side of temptation, this book shows how God uses temptation for our good. Patterson blends fresh style, humor, and scholarly insight to produce a helpful guide for beating temptation and coming out the better for it. (Leader's guide available—#39977.)

The Morality Maze (41010). This book serves as a roadmap through the confusing maze of conflicting opinions. There are some absolutes regarding morality, and Patterson helps you choose in harmony with them. (Leader's Guide available—#41011.)

Wonders in the Midst (40076). Here Patterson gives you a look at the major events and people in early Hebrew history. His look at God's leading through the exodus and into Canaan provides many insights into God's leading today. (Leader's Guide available—#40077.)